Private Information Retrieval

Synthesis Lectures on Information Security, Privacy, & Trust

Editor
Elisa Bertino, *Purdue University*
Ravi Sandhu, *University of Texas, San Antonio*

The Synthesis Lectures Series on Information Security, Privacy, and Trust publishes 50- to 100-page publications on topics pertaining to all aspects of the theory and practice of Information Security, Privacy, and Trust. The scope largely follows the purview of premier computer security research journals such as ACM Transactions on Information and System Security, IEEE Transactions on Dependable and Secure Computing and Journal of Cryptology, and premier research conferences, such as ACM CCS, ACM SACMAT, ACM AsiaCCS, ACM CODASPY, IEEE Security and Privacy, IEEE Computer Security Foundations, ACSAC, ESORICS, Crypto, EuroCrypt and AsiaCrypt. In addition to the research topics typically covered in such journals and conferences, the series also solicits lectures on legal, policy, social, business, and economic issues addressed to a technical audience of scientists and engineers. Lectures on significant industry developments by leading practitioners are also solicited.

Private Information Retrieval
Xun Yi, Russell Paulet, and Elisa Bertino
2013

Privacy for Location-based Services
Gabriel Ghinita
2013

Enhancing Information Security and Privacy by Combining Biometrics with Cryptography
Sanjay G. Kanade, Dijana Petrovska-Delacrétaz, and Bernadette Dorizzi
2012

Analysis Techniques for Information Security
Anupam Datta, Somesh Jha, Ninghui Li, David Melski, and Thomas Reps
2010

Operating System Security
Trent Jaeger
2008

Private Information Retrieval

Xun Yi, Russell Paulet, and Elisa Bertino

ISBN: 978-3-031-01209-9 paperback
ISBN: 978-3-031-02337-8 ebook

DOI 10.1007/978-3-031-02337-8

A Publication in the Springer series
SYNTHESIS LECTURES ON INFORMATION SECURITY, PRIVACY, & TRUST

Lecture #5
Series Editors: Elisa Bertino, *Purdue University*
Ravi Sandhu, *University of Texas, San Antonio*
Series ISSN
Synthesis Lectures on Information Security, Privacy, & Trust
Print 1945-9742 Electronic 1945-9750

Private Information Retrieval

Xun Yi
Victoria University, Australia

Russell Paulet
Victoria University, Australia

Elisa Bertino
Purdue University

SYNTHESIS LECTURES ON INFORMATION SECURITY, PRIVACY, & TRUST #5

ABSTRACT

This book deals with Private Information Retrieval (PIR), a technique allowing a user to retrieve an element from a server in possession of a database without revealing to the server which element is retrieved. PIR has been widely applied to protect the privacy of the user in querying a service provider on the Internet. For example, by PIR, one can query a location-based service provider about the nearest car park without revealing his location to the server.

The first PIR approach was introduced by Chor, Goldreich, Kushilevitz and Sudan in 1995 in a multi-server setting, where the user retrieves information from multiple database servers, each of which has a copy of the same database. To ensure user privacy in the multi-server setting, the servers must be trusted not to collude. In 1997, Kushilevitz and Ostrovsky constructed the first single-database PIR. Since then, many efficient PIR solutions have been discovered.

Beginning with a thorough survey of single-database PIR techniques, this text focuses on the latest technologies and applications in the field of PIR. The main categories are illustrated with recently proposed PIR-based solutions by the authors.

Because of the latest treatment of the topic, this text will be highly beneficial to researchers and industry professionals in information security and privacy.

KEYWORDS

private information retrieval, oblivious transfer, homomorphic encryption, private data warehouse queries, private location-based queries

Contents

Preface

Since 1994, the Internet has expanded to serve millions of users and a multitude of purposes worldwide and has become a powerful platform that has changed forever the way we do business and communicate. Recently, two innovations, social networks and mobile technology, have marked the Internet evolution and changed the way people use the Internet. In social networks, people have found a new way to communicate. Since its creation in 2004, Facebook has grown into a worldwide network of nearly 1 billion subscribers. Mobile technology, on the other hand, has made possible a much greater reach of the Internet, increasing the number of Internet users everywhere.

The Internet has become the universal source of information for millions of people, at home, at school, and at work. To utilize such universal source, a user usually needs to issue some queries to a service provider. An important category of such queries is represented by location-based queries by requiring as input, among other parameters, the user location; what are the restaurants close to my current location is an example of such queries? A major issue with such queries, as well as other categories of queries, is that they may harm the user's privacy.

On August 4, 2006, AOL Research released a compressed text file on one of its websites containing twenty million search keywords for over 650,000 users over a three-month period, intended for research purposes. AOL themselves did not identify users in the report. However, personally identifiable information was present in many of the queries, and as the queries were attributed by AOL to particular user accounts, identified numerically, an individual could be identified and matched to his/her account and search history by such information. The *New York Times* was able to locate an individual from the released and anonymized search records by cross referencing them with phonebook listings. This privacy breach was widely reported.

The use of Internet services has thus raised privacy concerns. The fundamental issue is that a user in order to ask for a service may need to disclose personal information. Very often just looking at what a user is looking for from an information source, like the Internet, can reveal sensitive information about the user. To protect user privacy is thus crucial that users are able to privately retrieve information. This requirement can be envisioned as making possible for a user Alice to retrieve an item from a database server without revealing to the database server which item has been retrieved. A trivial solution is for Alice to retrieve the entire database, but this approach may incur enormous communication cost or may not be in line with the business interests of the database owner. Private Information Retrieval (PIR) is able to provide non-trivial solutions to this kind of problem.

PIR allows a user to retrieve an item from a server in possession of a database without revealing to the server which item is retrieved. The first PIR approach was introduced by Chor,

Goldreich, Kushilevitz and Sudan in 1995 in a multi-server setting, where the user retrieves information from multiple database servers, each of which has a copy of the same database. To ensure user privacy in the multi-server setting, the servers must be trusted not to collude. In 1997, Kushilevitz and Ostrovsky constructed the first single-database PIR. Since then, many efficient solutions have been discovered.

Homomorphic encryption techniques are often very natural ways to construct PIR. For example, the PIR approach by Kushilevitz and Ostrovsky is based on the Goldwasser-Micali homomorphic encryption. A generic method to construct single-database PIR from a homomorphic encryption scheme was given by Ostrovsky and Skeith. These underlying encryption schemes allow homomorphic computation of only one operation (either addition or multiplication) on plaintexts. In 2009, Gentry constructed the first fully homomorphic encryption (FHE) scheme using lattice-based cryptography. FHE allows homomorphic computation of two operations (both addition and multiplication) of plaintexts. Motivated by recent breakthroughs in FHE, Yi, Kaosar, Paulet and Bertino proposed single-database PIR and Private Block Retrieval (PBR) protocols from FHE. Their solution is conceptually simpler than any existing PIR and more efficient in terms of computation complexity.

Publicly accessible data warehouses are an indispensable resource for data analysis. But they also pose a significant risk to the privacy of the clients, since a data warehouse operator may follow the client's queries and infer what the client is interested in. PIR techniques allow the client to retrieve a cell from a data warehouse without revealing to the operator which cell is retrieved. However, PIR cannot be used to hide Online Analytical Processing (OLAP) operations performed by the client, which may disclose the client's interest. Yi, Paulet and Bertino developed a solution for private data warehouse queries on the basis of the Boneh-Goh-Nissim cryptosystem which allows one to evaluate any multi-variate polynomial of total degree 2 on ciphertexts. By their solution, the client can perform OLAP operations on the data warehouse and retrieve one (or more) cell without revealing any information about which cell is selected.

Location-Based Services (LBS) provide information and offer services to customers using geographic location data. LBS offer a number of useful applications, including real-time navigation software, location-based social networking services that allow customers to check in their locations, and geographically targeted search engine results. The majority of applications for LBS are used in mobile services. Location information collected from consumers can reveal far more than just a consumer's latitude and longitude. Knowing where a consumer is can reveal what the consumer is doing: attending a religious service or a support meeting, visiting a doctor's office, shopping for an engagement ring, playing hooky from work, or spending an evening at the corner bar. Several approaches addressing privacy of LBS have been proposed. Most of the approaches are however either very expensive or not secure. Paulet, Kaosar, Yi and Bertino proposed a new approach to overcome the drawbacks of previous approaches adopting a two stage strategy. Their first step is based on Oblivious Transfer and their second step is based on Private Information

Retrieval. Their approach achieves a secure solution for both parties, and is efficient and practical in many scenarios.

Xun Yi, Russell Paulet, and Elisa Bertino
August 2013

Acknowledgments

We would like to thank Professor Shouhuai Xu (Department of Computer Science, University of Texas at San Antonio) and Dr. Ning Shang (Qualcomm) for their valuable comments which have been very helpful for us to improve the lectures.

Xun Yi, Russell Paulet, and Elisa Bertino
August 2013

CHAPTER 1

Classic Private Information Retrieval

1.1 INTRODUCTION

Private information retrieval (PIR) protocol allows a user to retrieve the i-th bit of an n-bit database, without revealing to the database server the value of i. A trivial solution is for the user to retrieve the entire database, but this approach may incur enormous communication cost. A good PIR protocol is expected to have considerably lower communication complexity. Private Block Retrieval (PBR) is a natural and more practical extension of PIR in which, instead of retrieving only a single bit, the user retrieves a block of bits from the database.

PIR was first introduced by Chor, Goldreich, Kushilevitz and Sudan [24] in 1995 in a multi-server setting, where the user retrieves information from multiple database servers, each of which has a copy of the same database. To ensure user privacy in the multi-server setting, the servers must be trusted not to collude. In [24], Chor et al. have shown that if only a single database is used, n bits must be communicated in the information-theoretic sense, that is, the user's query gives absolutely no information about i. They have also shown that any PIR protocol can be converted to a PBR protocol.

In 1997, using the quadratic residue computational assumption, Kushilevitz and Ostrovsky [68] constructed a single-database PIR with communication complexity of $O(2^{\sqrt{\log n \log\log N}})$ which is less than $O(n^{\epsilon})$ for any $\epsilon > 0$, where N is the composite modulus. Their basic idea is viewing the database as a matrix $M = (x_{ij})_{s\times t}$ of bits. To retrieve the (a, b) entry of the matrix, the user sends to the database server a composite (hard-to-factor) modulus N and t randomly chosen integers $y_1, y_2, \cdots, y_t$ such that only y_a is not a quadratic residue modulo N, that is, $y_i \neq \alpha^2 (mod\ N)$ for any integer α. The server sends back $z_i = \prod_{j=1}^{t} y_j^{2-x_{ij}}\ (mod\ N)$ for $1 \leqslant i \leqslant s$. The user concludes that $x_{ij} = 0$ if z_a is a quadratic residuosity modulo N, and $x_{ij} = 1$ otherwise.

In 1999, Cachin, Micali and Stadler [18] constructed the first single-database PIR with poly-logarithmic communication complexity $O(\log^8 n)$. The security of their protocol is based on the Φ-hiding number-theoretic assumption, that is, it is hard to distinguish which of two primes divides $\phi(N)$ for the composite modulus N. Their basic idea is mapping each index i to a distinct prime p_i. To retrieve bit b_i from a database $B = b_1 b_2 \cdots b_n$, the user sends to the database server a composite (hard-to-factor) modulus N such that p_i divides $\phi(N)$ and a generator g with order divisible by p_i. The server sends back $r = g^P (mod\ N)$ where $P = \prod_j p_j^{b_j}$. The user concludes that $b_i = 1$ if r is a p_i-residue modulo N, otherwise, $b_i = 0$.

In 2000, Kushilevitz and Ostrovsky [69] constructed a PIR protocol with total communication complexity $n - \frac{cn}{2k} + O(k^2)$, where k is a security parameter and c is a constant. Their protocol is built on the Naor-Yung one-way 2-to-1 trapdoor permutations [81] and the Goldreich-Levin hard-core predicates [52]. Their basic idea is dividing an n-bit database into k-bit blocks and organizing the database into pairs of blocks, denoted by $z_{i,L}$ and $z_{i,R}$, where $i = 1, 2, \cdots, \frac{n}{2k}$. Suppose that the user wishes to retrieve $z_{s,L}$. The user sends to the database server the descriptions of one-way trapdoor permutations f_L and f_R, to which the user has the trapdoors. The server computes $f_L(z_{i,L})$ and $f_R(z_{i,R})$ for all i and returns these values to the user. With trapdoors, the user computes two possible pairs of pre-images $(z_{s,L}, z'_{s,L})$ and $(z_{s,R}, z'_{s,R})$. Next, the user sends the server two hardcore predicates r_L and r_R such that $r_L(z_{s,L}) \neq r_L(z'_{s,L})$, but $r_R(z_{s,R}) = r_R(z'_{s,R})$. The server responds with $r_L(z_{i,L}) \oplus r_R(z_{i,R})$ for all i. At the end, the user learns which pre-image is $z_{s,L}$ from $r_L(z_{s,L})$.

In 2005, Gentry and Ramzan [40] extended the single-database PIR protocol of Cachin et al. [18] to a PBR with communication complexity $O(\log^2 n)$, the current best bound for communication complexity. The security of their protocol is also based on the Φ-hiding assumption. Assume that an n-bit database B is partitioned into m blocks, each has ℓ bits, denoted as $B = C_1 \| C_2 \| \cdots \| C_m$. Their basic idea is associating C_i with a distinct small prime p_i, rather than associating a (largish) prime with each bit. The database server uses the Chinese Reminder Theorem to determine an integer e such that $e = C_i (mod\ p_i^{c_i})$ for $1 \leqslant i \leqslant m$, where c_i is the smallest integer such that $p_i^{c_i} \geqslant 2^\ell$. To retrieve block C_i, the user sends to the database server a composite (hard-to-factor) modulus N such that $p_i^{c_i}$ divides $\phi(N)$ and a generator g with order divisible by $p_i^{c_i}$. The server sends back $r = g^e (mod\ N)$. Let $q = order(g)/p_i^{c_i}$, then $order(g^q) = p_i^{c_i}$. Since p_i is a small prime, the user can compute the discrete logarithm $\log_{(g^q)}(r^q) = e(mod\ p_i^{c_i}) = C_i$ using the Pohlig-Hellman algorithm [94].

Like the original single-database PIR of Kushilevitz and Ostrovsky [68], Chang [21] and Lipmaa [71, 72] also constructed PIR protocols with communication complexity of $O(\log^2 n)$. The difference is that the former is based on the Goldwasser-Micali homomorphic encryption [53], but the latter is built on the Damgard-Jurik homomorphic encryption [30], a variant of the Paillier homomorphic encryption [90].

Since PIR was first introduced by Chor, Goldreich, Kushilevitz and Sudan [24] in 1995, lots of PIR protocols have been proposed in literature [38, 87]. Generally, PIR protocols can be classified into two categories: information-theoretical PIR protocols such as [6, 24, 25, 32] (assume that there are multiple non-cooperating servers, each having a copy of the database) and computational PIR protocols such as [18, 21, 40, 68, 69, 71, 72] (assume that the server is computationally bounded). There also exist some PIR protocols based on the trusted hardware [73, 99, 104] (assume that a trusted hardware exists in the server to respond to the user's query without revealing to the server any query information). In this lecture, we will focus on single-database PIR protocols and their applications.

Single-database PIR has a close connection to the notion of Oblivious Transfer (OT), introduced by Rabin [95] in 1981. A different variant of OT, called 1-out-of-2 OT, was introduced by Even, Goldreich and Lempel [37] in 1985 and, more generally, 1-out-of-n OT was considered in Brassard, Crepeau and Robert [16] in 1987. Informally, OT is a two-party protocol, where a sender with n messages $M_1, M_2, \cdots, M_n$ and a receiver with an index i $(1 \leqslant i \leqslant n)$ interact, and at the end of the protocol the receiver obtains M_i without learning anything about other messages, while the sender does not learn anything about the index i.

OT is different from PIR in that there is no communication complexity requirement (beyond being polynomially bounded) but, on the other hand, secrecy is required for both players, while for PIR it is required only for the user. Naor and Pinkas [82] have shown how to turn any PIR protocol into 1-out-of-n OT protocol with one invocation of a single-database PIR protocol and logarithmic number of invocations of 1-out-of-2 OT. DiCrescenzo, Malkin and Ostrovsky [29] showed that any single-database PIR protocol implies 1-out-of-n OT.

The rest of this chapter is as follows: We give the definition of the security model for PIR in Section 1.2 and describe some classic PIR protocols in Section 1.3. Next, we give the definition of the security model for OT in Section 1.4 and introduce some classic OT protocols in Section 1.5. Then we discuss the relationship between PIR and OT in Section 1.6. Conclusions are drawn in Section 1.7.

1.2 SECURITY MODEL FOR PRIVATE INFORMATION RETRIEVAL

Informally, a single-database PIR protocol is a two-party protocol, where a user retrieves the i-th bit from an n-bit database $DB = b_1 b_2 \cdots b_n$, without revealing to the database server the value of i. Formally, a single-database PIR protocol consists of three algorithms as in [18, 40].

(1) Query Generation (QG): Takes as input a security parameter k, the size n of the database, and the index i of a bit in the database, outputs a query Q and a secret s, denoted as $(Q, s) = \mathsf{QG}(n, i, 1^k)$.

(2) Response Generation (RG): Takes as input the security parameter k, the query Q and the database DB, outputs a response R, denoted as $R = \mathsf{RG}(DB, Q, 1^k)$.

(3) Response Retrieval (RR): Takes as input the security parameter k, the response R, the index i of the bit, the size n of the database, the query Q, and the secret s, output a bit b', denoted as $b' = \mathsf{RR}(n, i, (Q, s), R, 1^k)$.

The security of single-database PIR protocol can be defined with a game as follows.

Give an n-bit database $DB = b_1 b_2 \cdots b_n$. Consider the following game between an adversary (the database server) $\mathcal{A}$, and a challenger $\mathcal{C}$. The game consists of the following steps:

(1) The adversary $\mathcal{A}$ chooses two different indices $1 \leqslant i, j \leqslant n$ and sends them to $\mathcal{C}$.

(2) Let $\lambda_0 = i$ and $\lambda_1 = j$. The challenger $\mathcal{C}$ chooses a random bit $b \in \{0, 1\}$, and executes $\mathsf{QG}(n, \lambda_b, 1^k)$ to obtain (Q_b, s), and then sends Q_b back to $\mathcal{A}$.

(3) The adversary $\mathcal{A}$ can experiment with the code of Q_b in an arbitrary non-black-box way, and finally outputs $b' \in \{0, 1\}$.

The adversary wins the game if $b' = b$ and loses otherwise. We define the adversary $\mathcal{A}$'s advantage in this game to be

$$\mathsf{Adv}_{\mathcal{A}}(k) = |\mathsf{Pr}(b' = b) - 1/2|.$$

Definition 1.1 **(Security Definition)** A single-database PIR protocol is semantically secure if for any probabilistic polynomial time (PPT) adversary $\mathcal{A}$, we have that $\mathsf{Adv}_{\mathcal{A}}(k)$ is a negligible function, where the probability is taken over coin-tosses of the challenger and the adversary.

Similarly, a single-database private block retrieval (PBR) protocol can be defined by viewing the n-bit database as $DB = B_1 \| B_2 \| \cdots \| B_m$, where B_i is a block with n/m bits.

Definition 1.2 **(Correctness)** A single-database PIR protocol is correct if, for any security parameter k, any database DB with any size n, and any index i for $1 \leqslant i \leqslant n$, $b_i = \mathsf{RR}(n, i, (Q, s), R, 1^k)$ holds, where $(Q, s) = \mathsf{QG}(n, i, 1^k)$ and $R = \mathsf{RG}(DB, Q, 1^k)$.

In simple terms, the correctness definition means that for every query Q, the correct bit/block is retrieved. While, the security definition means that for any two queries Q_1, Q_2, with indices i, j respectively, an adversary cannot distinguish them from one another with probability greater than $\frac{1}{2}$. With this general definition of a PIR protocol in mind, we give some notable constructions from the literature.

1.3 PRIVATE INFORMATION RETRIEVAL PROTOCOLS

1.3.1 KUSHILEVITZ-OSTROVSKY PIR PROTOCOL

The first single-database computational PIR protocol to achieve communication complexity less than n was created in 1997 by Kushilevitz and Ostrovsky [68]. It is built on Goldwasser-Micali cryptosystem [53], whose security is based on the problem of determining a quadratic residue modulo N, where N is a hard-to-factor integer.

Quadratic Residue

In number theory, an integer a is called a quadratic residue modulo N if it is congruent to a perfect square modulo N, i.e., if there exists an integer x such that:

$$x^2 = a(mod\ N) \tag{1.1}$$

Otherwise, a is called a quadratic nonresidue modulo N.

Goldwasser-Micali Cryptosystem

Goldwasser-Micali cryptosystem was the earliest example of what is known as probabilistic encryption [53], which in this context means that there are many ciphertexts that encode the same message. In this case, we are encoding bit by bit, so the ciphertext space is larger than the message space. We define a function $Q(a)$ such that it returns 1 if a is a quadratic nonresidue and 0 otherwise. Then Goldwasser-Micali cryptosystem can be described as follows:

Keygen The key generation procedure begins with selecting two $k/2$-bit primes p, q and computing the product $N = pq$. Then, an integer $a \in \mathbb{Z}_n$ is chosen such that it is a quadratic nonresidue. The public key is $[N, a]$, while the the private key is $[p, q]$.

Encryption Compute the encryption of message $m \in \{0, 1\}$ as $E(m) = a^m r^2 \ (mod \ N)$, where $r \in \mathbb{Z}_n^*$ is chosen at random. If $m = 0$, $E(m) = x^2 \ (mod \ N)$ is a quadratic residue. If $m = 1$, $E(m)$ is a quadratic nonresidue.

Decryption Compute the decryption of ciphertext c as $D(c) = Q(c)$.

This scheme has additively homomorphic mod 2 property. Equivalently, this can be seen as the XOR operation on binary digits or bits. Given encryptions of bits b_1, b_2 as $E(b_1)$ and $E(b_2)$, we have the following homomorphism demonstrated by

$$E(b_1)E(b_2) = a^{b_1} r_1^2 a^{b_2} r_2^2 = a^{b_1+b_2}(r_1 r_2)^2 = E(b_1 \oplus b_2) \tag{1.2}$$

Kushilevitz-Ostrovsky PIR Protocol

Based on the above Goldwasser-Micali cryptosystem, Kushilevitz-Ostrovsky PIR protocol is constructed as follows:

In the protocol, the database is represented as two-dimensional matrix $M_{s \times t} = (m_{i,j})$ of bits. The user desires to retrieve the bit at position (i^*, j^*).

Query Generation The user creates a k-bit number $N = pq$, where p, q are two $k/2$-bit primes and chooses a quadratic nonresidue a. The user then computes t numbers $x_1, x_2, \cdots, x_t$, where $x_{j*} = a r_{j*}^2 (mod \ N)$ is a quadratic nonresidue and $x_j = r_j^2 (mod \ N)$, for $j \neq j^*$, is a quadratic residue, r_j is a random number. In other words, $x_1, x_2, \cdots, x_t$ are encryptions of $0, \cdots, 1, \cdots, 0$, where all bits are 0 except that the bit at j^* position is 1. The user sends $[N, x_1, x_2, \cdots, x_t]$ to the database server.

Response Generation For every row i, the server computes $z_i = \prod_{j=1}^{t} y_{i,j}$, where

$$y_{i,j} = \begin{cases} x_j^2 & \text{if } m_{i,j} = 0 \\ x_j & \text{if } m_{i,j} \neq 0 \end{cases} \tag{1.3}$$

The s numbers $[z_1, z_2, \cdots, z_s]$ are sent to the user.

Response Retrieval The user recovers the bit by analyzing the i^*-th integer z_{i*}; the bit at (i^*, j^*) (i.e., $m_{i,j}$) is 0 if z_{i*} is a quadratic residue, and a 1 otherwise. Since the factorization of N is known, this can be done efficiently.

Kushilevitz-Ostrovsky PIR protocol is correct. When $j \neq j^*$, x_j is a quadratic residue and thus $y_{i*,j} = x_j^2$ or x_j is still a quadratic residue. This means that whether $z_{i*} = \prod_{j=1}^{t} y_{i*,j}$ is a quadratic residue or not depends on $y_{i*,j*}$ only. If $m_{i,j} = 0$, $y_{i*,j*} = x_{j*}^2$ is a quadratic residue. If $m_{i,j} = 1$, $y_{i*,j*} = x_{j*}$ is a quadratic nonresidue. Therefore, z_{i*} is a quadratic residue if and only if $m_{i,j} = 0$, and z_{i*} is a quadratic nonresidue if and only if $m_{i,j} = 1$.

Kushilevitz-Ostrovsky PIR protocol is built on Goldwasser-Micali cryptosystem. As long as Goldwasser-Micali cryptosystem is a secure public key encryption scheme, Kushilevitz-Ostrovsky PIR protocol is secure. In addition, the communication complexity of Kushilevitz-Ostrovsky PIR protocol is $O(n^{1/2} \log n)$, where n is the size (number of bits) in the database. It is improved to $O(n^{\epsilon} \log n)$ (where ϵ is any constant) in a recursive version of Kushilevitz-Ostrovsky PIR protocol [68].

1.3.2 CHANG PIR PROTOCOL

Chang PIR protocol [21] is built on Paillier cryptosystem [90], which is based on the decisional composite residuosity assumption (DCRA).

Decisional Composite Residuosity Assumption

Decisional Composite Residuosity Assumption (DCRA) states that given a composite N and an integer y, it is hard to decide whether y is the N-residue modulo N^2 or not, i.e., whether there exists x such that

$$y = x^N (mod\ N^2) \tag{1.4}$$

Paillier Cryptosystem

Paillier cryptosystem [90] can be seen as a ElGamal cryptosystem with some of the characteristics of the RSA cryptosystem. It can be described as follows.

Keygen Choose two prime numbers p and q and compute the product $N = pq$. Compute $\lambda = \phi(N) = (p-1)(q-1)$ and set $g = 1 + N$. The public key is N and the private key is λ.

Encryption Compute the encryption of message m as $E(m) = g^m \cdot r^N\ (mod\ N^2)$, where r is randomly chosen from $\mathbb{Z}_{N^2}^*$.

Decryption Compute the decryption of ciphertext c as

$$D(c) = \frac{[c^{\lambda}\ (mod\ N^2)] - 1}{N} \cdot \lambda^{-1}\ (mod\ N) \tag{1.5}$$

The correctness of Paillier cryptosystem can be verified using the Binomial Theorem. When we raise the ciphertext $c = g^m \cdot r^N (mod\ N^2)$ to the power of λ, we get $c^{\lambda} = (g^m \cdot r^N)^{\lambda} =$

$(g^m)^\lambda \cdot (r^N)^\lambda = g^{m\lambda} \cdot 1 = g^{m\lambda} (mod\ N^2)$. Note that $\phi(N^2) = N\lambda$. It remains to see what happens when $g = 1 + N$ is raised by $m\lambda$. Because

$$c^\lambda = g^{m\lambda} = (N+1)^{m\lambda} = 1 + mN\lambda + dN^2 = 1 + mN\lambda\ (mod\ N^2) \tag{1.6}$$

where d is an integer, we have $\frac{[c^\lambda\ (mod\ N^2)]-1}{N} \cdot \lambda^{-1}\ (mod\ N) = m$.

Paillier cryptosystem is additively homomorphic. If we have two ciphertexts as $E(m_1) = g^{m_1} r_1^N$ and $E(m_2) = g^{m_1} r_2^N$, where m_1, m_2 are two messages, we have

$$E(m_1)E(m_2) = (g^{m_1} r_1^N)(g^{m_1} r_2^N) = g^{m_1+m_2}(r_1 r_2)^N = E(m_1 + m_2) \tag{1.7}$$

Paillier cryptosystem was introduced considerably after the birth of public key cryptography, but it has grown with popularity ever since—especially because of its attractive homomorphic property. It is related to the Goldwasser-Micali cryptosystem [53] and its subsequent extensions [8, 80, 85]. The most notable feature, when compared to previous cryptosystems, is its straightforward decryption.

Chang PIR Protocol

Chang PIR protocol [21] arranges the database into a square matrix (or a cube) and then "encrypts" the indices to retrieve the specified bit. For this exposition, we arrange the database as a matrix $M_{s\times s} = (m_{i,j})$ of zeros and ones. Let I be an indicating function such that

$$I(x, y) = \begin{cases} 1 & \text{if } x = y \\ 0 & \text{otherwise} \end{cases} \tag{1.8}$$

Also, let $E(m)$ be the Paillier encryption algorithm for message m and let $D(c)$ be the corresponding decryption algorithm for ciphertext c, where there is an implicit random input supplied to the encryption algorithm. Suppose the user wishes to retrieve the bit at position (i^*, j^*), Chang PIR protocol can be described as follows.

Query Generation The user creates a query as $[a_t, b_t] = [E(I(t, i^*)), E(I(t, j^*))]$ for $t \in \{1, 2, \cdots, s\}$ and sends the query to the server.

Response Generation Upon receiving the user's query, the server computes

$$w_i = \prod_{j=1}^{s} b_j{}^{m(i,j)} (mod\ N^2) \tag{1.9}$$

for $i \in \{1, 2, \cdots, s\}$. The server then splits each w_i by letting $u_i, v_i \in \mathbb{Z}_N$ such that $w_i = u_i N + v_i$ for $i \in \{1, 2, \cdots, s\}$ and computes

$$u = \prod_{i=1}^{s} a_i{}^{u_i} (mod\ N^2) \tag{1.10}$$

$$v = \prod_{i=1}^{s} a_i{}^{v_i} (mod\ N^2) \tag{1.11}$$

and replies (u, v) to the user.

Response Retrieval The user reconstructs as $m(i^*, , j^*) = D(D(u)N + D(v))$.

Chang PIR protocol is correct. Because of the additively homomorphic property of Paillier cryptosystem, each w_i is equal to $E(m(i, j^*))$ and thus w_{i*} is equal to $E(m(i^*, j^*))$. In addition, $u = E(u_{i*})$ and $v = E(v_{i*})$ and thus $D(u)N + D(v) = u_{i*}N + v_{i*} = w_{i*} = E(m_{i*,j*})$. Therefore, $m_{i*,j*} = D(D(u)N + D(v))$.

The security of Chang PIR protocol is built on the security of Paillier cryptosystem. As long as Paillier cryptosystem is a secure public key encryption scheme, Chang PIR protocol is secure. In addition, the communication complexity of Chang PIR protocol is $O(n^{\epsilon} \log n)$, where n is the size of the database.

1.3.3 GENTRY-RAZMAN PIR PROTOCOL

Gentry PIR protocol [40] is based on a relatively new computational hardness assumption, which is known as the phi-hiding assumption (Φ-hiding assumption). The first use of this assumption in PIR was by [18], where only one bit could be retrieved per round. This was extended in Gentry PIR protocol [40], to consider blocks instead of single bits.

Phi-Hiding Assumption

Phi-Hiding assumption or Φ-hiding assumption is an assumption about the difficulty of finding small factors of $\phi(N)$ where N is a number whose factorization is unknown, and ϕ is Euler's totient function. It is commonly believed that if N is the product of two large primes, then calculating $\phi(N)$ is currently computationally infeasible, this assumption is required for the security of the RSA Cryptosystem. The Φ-Hiding assumption is a stronger assumption, namely that if p and q are small primes exactly one of which divides $\phi(N)$, there is no polynomial-time algorithm which can distinguish which of the primes p and q divides $\phi(N)$ with probability significantly greater than 1/2.

Gentry-Razman PIR Protocol

Gentry-Razman PIR protocol divides the database into m distinct blocks $DB = C_1||C_2||\cdots||C_m$, where each C_i is represented by an integer less than ℓ bits and chooses a set $S = \{\pi_i = p_1^{c_1}, \cdots, \pi_m = p_m^{c_m}\}$, where each prime power pair is coprime, i.e., $GCD(\pi_i, \pi_j) = 1$ for $1 \leqslant i, j \leqslant m$ (GCD stands for Greatest Common Divisor) and c_i is the smallest integer such that $\pi_i = p_i^{c_i} > 2^{\ell}$ for $1 \leqslant i \leqslant m$. The server then finds an integer e, such that $e = C_j\ (mod\ \pi_j)$ for $1 \leqslant j \leqslant m$, using the Chinese Remainder Theorem. With this in mind, we detail the steps of Gentry-Razman PIR protocol.

Query Generation The user decides to download the block C_i and constructs a query by using the corresponding π_i as follows. The user constructs a group G and a "quasi-generator" g, such that $|G| = q\pi_i$ for some $q \in \mathbb{Z}$. In other words π_i divides the order of the group. The user outputs the description of the group (G, g), but computes $h = g^q$ for later use.

Response Generation After receiving the description of the group (G, g), the server computes $g_e = g^e \in G$ and replies it to the user.

Response Retrieval Upon receiving g_e, the user computes $h_e = g_e^q$. Then the user determines C_i as the discrete logarithm of h_e base h, i.e., $C_i = \log_h h_e$.

Gentry-Razman PIR protocol is correct. Because $e = C_i (mod\ \pi_i)$, we have $h_e = g_e^q = g^{eq} = g^{C_i q} = (g^q)^{C_i} = h^{C_i}$. Therefore, $C_i = log_h h_e$.

In general, the discrete logarithm problem is considered hard. In most cases, we require this problem to be computationally intractable for security reasons. But in this case, we require this problem to be tractable, or computable with contemporary technology. The discrete logarithm can be accelerated using Pohlig-Hellman algorithm [94]. This algorithm is very efficient, compared with a brute force algorithm, when we know the order of the group. In Gentry-Razman PIR protocol, we know the order of the group, i.e., $\pi_i = p_i^{c_i}$. Let $C_i = a_0 + a_1 p_i + \cdots + a_{c_i - 1} p_i^{c_i - 1}$, where $0 \leqslant a_i \leqslant p_i - 1$. Since $h_e = h^{C_i}$, we have $h_e^{p_i^{c_i-1}} = h^{C_i p_i^{c_i-1}} = h^{a_0 p_i^{c_i-1}}$. Because $0 \leqslant a_0 \leqslant p_i - 1$ and p_i is a small prime, it is not hard to determine a_0 by brute force. After that, we obtain $h_e h^{-a_0} = h^{C_i - a_0}$ and then $(h_e h^{-a_0})^{p_i^{c_i-2}} = (h^{C_i - a_0})^{p_i^{c_i-2}} = h^{a_1 p_i^{c_i-1}}$. By brute force, we can determine a_1. In the same way, we can determine other coefficients.

Gentry-Razman PIR protocol needs to construct a hidden group H within a larger group G, of order π_i, i.e., embedding π_i in the order of G. This can be achieved by computing two integers $Q_0 = 2q_0\pi_i + 1$ and $Q_1 = 2dq_1 + 1$, where q_0, q_1 are prime numbers, π_i is the prime power referencing the block at i, and d is suitable random integer. If Q_0, Q_1 are also prime numbers, we can compute a modulus $N = Q_0 Q_1$, where the order of the group is $\phi(N) = (Q_0 - 1)(Q_1 - 1)$, which contains π_i as a factor. When an element of group G is raised to the power of integer $q = |G|/\pi$, this reduces it to an element of group H. Thus it remains to compute the discrete logarithm of group H.

The security of Gentry-Razman PIR protocol is based on Phi-hiding assumption. As long as Phi-hiding problem is hard, Gentry-Razman PIR protocol is secure. In addition, the communication complexity of Gentry-Razman PIR protocol is $O(\log^2 n)$, the current best bound for communication complexity in PIR protocols.

1.4 SECURITY MODEL FOR OBLIVIOUS TRANSFER

The concept of Oblivious Transfer (OT) [95] has an intimate relationship with PIR.[1] Even though chronologically, oblivious transfer actually pre-dates PIR. OT can be considered a stronger version of PIR [87]. In the case where there are multiple non-colluding databases this is termed Symmetric Private Information Retrieval (sPIR) [39, 82].[2]

The original probability transfer presented by Rabin was extended to provide a deterministic result [37], with the introduction of the 1-out-of-2 oblivious transfer denoted by OT_1^2. These two protocols were proven to be fundamentally the same [28]. The OT_1^2 primitive can be easily extended to 1-out-of-n oblivious transfer, denoted by a similar manner as OT_1^n [16]. In [16], an OT_1^n was described under the name *all-or-nothing disclosure of secrets*. This protocol was extended by [102], where the main contribution is a zero-knowledge proof.

Oblivious transfer is an interactive protocol between two algorithms Alice and Bob. First, let us focus our attention on the most simple case of the 1-out-of-2 oblivious transfer OT_1^2. In the simplest case, Bob has two bits b_0, b_1, while Alice has a selection bit $b \in \{0, 1\}$. At the conclusion of the protocol Alice should learn b_c and nothing about $b_{\overline{c}}$ where $\overline{c} = 1 - c$. Additionally, Bob should learn absolutely nothing at the end of the protocol. A more advanced and general case is where Bob has n bit strings $x_0, x_1, \cdots, x_n$ and Alice can learn x_i where $0 \leqslant i \leqslant n$ is Alice's chosen index. In this scenario, Alice learns only x_i and Bob learns nothing about i. This general construction is known as a 1-out-of-n scheme OT_1^n. Obviously, we can achieve a k-out-of-n OT_k^n protocol by invoking a OT_1^n protocol k times.

In order to prove security for oblivious transfer protocols we cannot completely reuse the indistinguishability model from PIR, since there is an additional requirement that the receiver cannot learn any more than allowed. Thus we need to introduce the concept of real-world/ideal-world simulation. This is where we consider two executions of the same protocol. One execution is in the real world, while another is in the ideal world. If we can prove that the two executions are the same (indistinguishable), then the protocol is secure, by definition of the ideal-world implementation.

Within this security framework, we consider a static adversary $\mathcal{A}$. This adversary is allowed to corrupt only one out of the two honest parties engaged in the OT protocol and is allowed to deviate from the protocol. This attack must occur at the beginning of the protocol and cannot be changed for the duration of the protocol. We now give the definitions for the receiver's security and senders security, respectively. These definitions are in terms of k out of n adaptive oblivious transfer $OT_{k\times 1}^n$, as opposed to regular k out of n oblivious transfer OT_k^n. From a security viewpoint, they are essentially the same. What differs is the ability, in adaptive OT, to perform queries without downloading a large amount of data with each query.

[1]The idea was independently formulated by Wiesner [105], which was built on the theory of quantum mechanics. But the basic idea is the same.

[2]In the case of single-database Symmetric Private Information Retrieval, this is equivalent to oblivious transfer, with the added requirement of being communicationally efficient.

An adaptive OT protocol $OT^n_{k\times 1}$ is defined as a two stage process: an initialization phase and a transfer phase. In the first phase, a commitment of keys is transferred from the server to the client, which takes $O(n)$ work, where n is the number of elements. In the second phase, these commitments are adaptively queried and with each query, only one message is revealed. With this description in mind, we give the security definitions for adaptive oblivious transfer.

Definition 1.3 Client's Security (Indistinguishability). In a $OT^n_{k\times 1}$ protocol, for any step $1 \leqslant t \leqslant k$, for any previous items $i_1, \cdots, i_{t-1}$ that the receiver (i.e., the client) has obtained in the first $t-1$ transfers, for any $1 \leqslant i_t, i'_t \leqslant n$ and for any probabilistic polynomial time machine $\mathcal{B}'$ executing the server's part, the views that $\mathcal{B}'$ sees in case the client tries to obtain x_{i_t} and in the case the client tries to obtain $x_{i'_t}$ are computationally indistinguishable given $x_1, x_2, \cdots, x_n$.

Definition 1.4 Server's Security (Comparison with Ideal Model). We compare a $OT^n_{k\times 1}$ protocol to the *ideal implementation*, using a trusted third party C that gets the server's input $x_1, x_2, \cdots, x_n$ and the client's request i and gives the client the data element x_i he/she has requested. For every probabilistic polynomial-time machine $\mathcal{A}'$ substituting the receiver (i.e., the client), there exists a probabilistic polynomial-time machine $\mathcal{A}''$ that plays the receiver's role in the ideal model such that the outputs of $\mathcal{A}'$ and $\mathcal{A}''$ are computationally indistinguishable. This implies that except for x_i that the client has learned the rest of $x_1, x_2, \cdots, x_n$ are semantically secure.

The above definitions are first given in [83]. The client's security is very similar to the definition of PIR security. That is given two queries from the receiver, the sender (i.e, the server) cannot (in polynomial time) distinguish them. The security for the sender is more difficult and we have to use the simulation model. This is because we must prevent a malicious receiver from learning more information about the sender's database by deviating from the protocol.

To show that an OT protocol is secure against such an attack, one should create an ideal-world implementation of the receiver that uses a trusted third party to perform key tasks of the protocol. If one can show that a real-world implementation is statistically equivalent, then he can claim that the OT protocol is secure.

1.5 OBLIVIOUS TRANSFER PROTOCOLS

1.5.1 EVEN-GOLDREICH-LEMPEL OT^2_1 PROTOCOL

Even et al.'s protocol [37] is a 1-out-of-2 oblivious transfer protocol OT^2_1, where the sender has two messages m_0 and m_1, and the receiver has a bit b, and the receiver wishes to receive m_b, without the sender learning b, while the sender wants to ensure that the receiver receives only one of the two messages. Even et al.'s protocol is general, but can be instantiated using the well-known RSA cryptosystem.

RSA

The RSA is defined by three algorithms: key generation, encryption, and decryption. The key generation algorithm selects two primes p and q that are essentially the same size and computes the product $N = pq$. Then it chooses a random e such that $gcd(e, \phi(N)) = 1$. It then finds a d where $d = e^{-1} \ (mod\ N)$. It outputs (e, N) as the public key pk and (d, N) as the secret key sk.

The encryption algorithm takes a message m and the public key (e, N) and computes ciphertext c as $c = m^e \ (mod\ N)$. Whereas the decryption algorithm takes a ciphertext c and the private key (d, N) and computes a message m' as $m' = c^d \ (mod\ N)$. Correctness of decryption follows from the consequence of Euler's Theorem: $x^{\phi(N)} = 1 \ (mod\ N)$ for any $x \in \mathbb{Z}_N^*(= \{1, 2, \cdots, N-1\})$.

The security of RSA is built on two mathematical problems: the problem of factoring large numbers and the RSA problem. Full decryption of an RSA ciphertext is thought to be infeasible on the assumption that both of these problems are hard. Providing security against partial decryption may require the addition of a secure padding scheme.

The RSA problem is defined as the task of taking eth roots modulo a composite N: recovering a value m such that $c = m^e (mod\ N)$, where (e, N) is an RSA public key and c is an RSA ciphertext. Currently the most promising approach to solving the RSA problem is to factor the modulus N. With the ability to recover prime factors, an attacker can compute the secret exponent d from a public key (e, N), then decrypt c using the standard procedure. To accomplish this, an attacker factors N into p and q, and computes $(p-1)(q-1)$ which allows the determination of d from e. No polynomial-time method for factoring large integers on a classical computer has yet been found, but it has not been proven that none exists.

Even-Goldreich-Lempel OT_1^2 Protocol

In Even-Goldreich-Lempel OT_1^2 protocol[37], there exist two parties: Alice and Bob, where Alice plays the role of the sender, while Bob plays the role of the receiver.

1. Alice generates an instance of the RSA cryptosystem and sends the public key e, N to Bob.

2. Alice chooses two random integers $x_0, x_1 \in \mathbb{Z}_N^*$ and sends to Bob.

3. Bob selects one of the two integers and computes $y = x_b + r^e \ (mod\ N)$, where $b \in \{0, 1\}$, e is the public key of Alice, and $r \in \mathbb{Z}_N^*$ is chosen randomly. Bob sends y to Alice.

4. Alice computes two possible r values as $r_0 = (y - x_0)^d \ (mod\ N)$ and $r_1 = (y - x_1)^d \ (mod\ N)$, where d is the private key of Alice. Alice sends $m_0' = m_0 + r_0$ and $m_1' = m_1 + r_1$ to Bob.

5. Bob either computes $m_0 = m_0' - r$ or $m_1 = m_1' - r$ based on his choice of x_b.

Even-Goldreich-Lempel OT_1^2 protocol is correct and secure.

If $b = 0$, then $r_0 = (y - x_0)^d = (x_0 + r^e - x_0)^d = r$ and thus Bob can obtain $m'_0 - r = m_0 + r_0 - r = m_0$. However, because $m'_1 + r_1 = m_1 + (y - x_1)^d = m_1 + (x_0 + r^e - x_1)^d$ and Bob does not know d, he cannot find out m_1 from m'_1.

If $b = 1$, then $r_1 = (y - x_1)^d = (x_1 + r^e - x_1)^d = r$ and thus Bob can obtain $m'_1 - r = m_1 + r_1 - r = m_1$. However, because $m'_0 = m_0 + r_0 = m_0 + (y - x_0)^d = m_0 + (x_1 + r^e - x_0)^d$ and Bob does not know d, he can find out m_0 from m'_0.

All above computations are modulo N. Furthermore, due to the random r chosen by Bob in $y = x_b + r^e \ (mod\ N)$, Alice cannot determine which message Bob received.

This demonstrates the client and server security, the two security requirements for oblivious transfer, of Even-Goldreich-Lempel OT_1^2 protocol.

Note that both m_0 and m_1 can be determined by Bob if m_0 and m_1 are small integers. For example, in case of $b = 0$, Bob can determine m_1 by testing if $(m'_1 - m_1)^e = y - x_1$ for all possible m_1. Providing security against the attack may require the addition of a secure padding scheme as RSA.

1.5.2 NAOR-PINKAS OT_1^n PROTOCOL

Naor and Pinkas gave a constructions of a 1-out-of-n OT protocol [82]. The protocol is based on a family of pseudo-random functions.

Pseudo-Random Function

A Pseudo-Random Function (PRF) is an efficient (i.e., computable in polynomial time) deterministic function that maps two distinct sets (domain and range) on the basis of a key. Essentially a true random function would just be composed of a look-up table filled with random entries. However, in practice a PRF has only one input d (domain) and a hidden random seed K (key) which when run multiple times with the same input, always outputs the same value. Nonetheless, given an arbitrary input the output looks random due to the random seed.

A PRF is considered to be good if its behavior is indistinguishable from a true random function. Therefore, given a true random function and a PRF, there should be no efficient method of determining if the output was produced by a true random function or the PRF.

Naor-Pinkas OT_1^n Protocol

Naor-Pinkas OT_1^n Protocol [82] is based on a family of pseudo-random functions, denoted as $\{F_K : \{0,1\}^m \mapsto \{0,1\}^m | K \in \{0,1\}^t\}$, where K stands for the key for the function.

In Naor-Pinkas OT_1^n protocol, the server B input $X_1, X_2, \cdots, X_n$, where $X_I \in \{0,1\}^m$ and $N = 2^\ell$, the client A would like to learn X_I. The protocol is described as follows.

1. The server creates ℓ pairs of keys randomly

$$(K_1^0, K_1^1), (K_2^0, K_2^1), \cdots, (K_\ell^0, K_\ell^1)$$

where for all j in the range $1 \leqslant j \leqslant \ell$ and $b \in \{0, 1\}$, each K_j^b is a t-bit key input to the pseudo-random function F_K. Denote $(i_1, i_2, \cdots, i_\ell)$ as the bits of I for all $1 \leqslant I \leqslant n$. The server computes

$$Y_I = X_I \oplus \bigoplus_{j=1}^{\ell} F_{K_j^{i_j}}(I) \tag{1.12}$$

2. The client and server interactively conduct a 1-out-of-2 OT for each $1 \leqslant j \leqslant \ell$ on each key pair (K_j^0, K_j^1). For instance, if the client wants to discover X_I, then they should choose $K_j^{i_j}$.

3. The server sends the client the set of strings $Y_1, Y_2, \cdots, Y_n$.

4. The client recovers X_I as $X_I = Y_I \oplus \bigoplus_{j=1}^{\ell} F_{K_j^{i_j}}(I)$.

Naor-Pinkas OT_1^n protocol is correct and secure. If $Y_I = X_I \oplus \bigoplus_{j=1}^{\ell} F_{K_j^{i_j}}(I)$, then $Y_I \oplus \bigoplus_{j=1}^{\ell} F_{K_j^{i_j}}(I) = X_I \oplus \bigoplus_{j=1}^{\ell} F_{K_j^{i_j}}(I) \oplus \bigoplus_{j=1}^{\ell} F_{K_j^{i_j}}(I) = X_I$. Therefore, the protocol is correct. The security of the protocol is built on the security of the underlying OT_1^2 protocols. If the underlying OT_1^2 protocols have client's security and server's security, Naor-Pinkas OT_1^n protocol has client's security and server's security as well.

1.5.3 NAOR-PINKAS $OT_{k\times 1}^n$ PROTOCOL

The construction of Naor-Pinkas $OT_{k\times 1}^n$ protocol [83] is built on the decisional Diffie–Hellman (DDH) assumption.

Decisional Diffie–Hellman Assumption

The decisional Diffie–Hellman (DDH) assumption is a computational hardness assumption about a certain problem involving discrete logarithms in cyclic groups. It is used as the basis to prove the security of many cryptographic protocols, most notably the ElGamal cryptosystem [36].

DDH assumption can be described as: given a cyclic group G and a generator g, it is computationally difficult to distinguish between two tuples in the form (g^a, g^b, g^{ab}) and (g^a, g^b, g^c), where a, b, c are taken from a suitable random distribution and the discrete logarithm problem is hard.

Naor-Pinkas $OT_{k\times 1}^n$ Protocol

Naor-Pinkas $OT_{k\times 1}^n$ protocol is divided into two stages. In the initialization phase, an array of encryption keys are generated and messages are encrypted with corresponding keys by the server. In the transfer phase the client and server interact such that the client learns k encryption keys (and no other), and the server cannot learn which keys were requested. With the k encryption keys, the client is able to decrypt k ciphertexts to obtain k messages.

Assume that G is a cyclic group with a generator g and the DDH assumption holds on G. The n database elements are arranged as a two-dimensional matrix $X_{1,1}, \cdots, X_{\sqrt{n},\sqrt{n}}$.

At the initialization phase, the server B chooses $2\sqrt{n}$ random keys $(R_1, R_2, ..., R_{\sqrt{n}})$ and $(C_1, C_2, ..., C_{\sqrt{n}})$, computes the key $K_{i,j} = g^{R_i C_j}$ and encrypts $X_{i,j}$ with the key $K_{i,j}$, denoted as $Y_{i,j} = E_{K_{i,j}}(X_{i,j})$, for $1 \leqslant i, j \leqslant \sqrt{n}$. Then the server sends $Y_{1,1}, \cdots, Y_{i,j}, \cdots Y_{\sqrt{n},\sqrt{n}}$ to the client.

In the transfer phase, the client A interacts with the server B as follows.

1. The server B selects two random elements $r_R, r_C \in G$ according to a suitable distribution.

2. The client A and server B execute a protocol $OT_1^{\sqrt{n}}$ for the tuple $(R_1 \cdot r_R, R_2 \cdot r_R, ..., R_{\sqrt{n}} \cdot r_R)$. If A wants to learn $X_{i,j}$, A should pick $R_i \cdot r_R$ from B.

3. The client A and server B execute a protocol $OT_1^{\sqrt{n}}$ for the tuple $(C_1 \cdot r_C, C_2 \cdot r_C, ..., C_{\sqrt{n}} \cdot r_C)$. If A wants to learn $X_{i,j}$, A should pick $C_j \cdot r_C$ from B.

4. The server B computes $\gamma = g^{r_R r_C}$ and sends γ to the client A.

5. The client A computes $K_{i,j}$ as
$$K_{i,j} = (\gamma)^{(R_i r_R) \cdot (C_j r_C)} = (g^{(r_R r_C)})^{(R_i r_R) \cdot (C_j r_C)} = g^{R_i C_j} \tag{1.13}$$

6. The client A uses $K_{i,j}$ to decrypt $Y_{i,j} = E_{K_{i,j}}(X_{i,j})$ to obtain $X_{i,j}$.

The above protocol is repeated for k times until the client receives k messages. In Naor-Pinkas $OT_{k\times 1}^n$ protocol, the $OT_1^{\sqrt{n}}$ protocol can be implemented by Naor-Pinkas OT_1^n protocol described in 1.5.2.

Based on Eq. (1.13), the client can clearly obtain k messages she wishes to retrieve in Naor-Pinkas $OT_{k\times 1}^n$ protocol. In other word, Naor-Pinkas $OT_{k\times 1}^n$ protocol is correct.

As for the complexity of the protocol, the initialization phase requires B to compute all n keys, i.e., to compute n modular exponentiations. Each transfer phase requires two invocations of an $OT_1^{\sqrt{n}}$ protocol, in which each requires $O(\sqrt{n})$ initialization work by B.

The client's security is guaranteed by the client's security of the $OT_1^{\sqrt{n}}$ protocols which do not disclose to B information about A's choices.

The server's security of B is guaranteed by the DDH assumption. If the client can retrieve more than k messages by running the protocol k times, the DDH problem can be solved. Therefore, as long as the DDH assumption holds on G, Naor-Pinkas $OT_{k\times 1}^n$ protocol has server's security.

The significance of Naor-Pinkas $OT_{k\times 1}^n$ protocol is that once the server's commitment of the database elements is initialized, the client can repeatedly (and efficiently) query the database at different locations. And after every invocation of the transfer protocol, the client can decide what to query next. This is in contrast with the naive approach where the client downloads k records in one transaction. In this case, the client needs to decide what elements they desire before they begin the protocol.

1.6 RELATIONSHIP BETWEEN PIR AND OT

Single-database PIR has a close connection to the notation of OT. OT is different from PIR in that there is no communication complexity requirement (beyond being polynomially bounded) but, on the other hand, privacy is required for both client and server, while for PIR, it is required only for the user. All OT definitions are shown to be equivalent [28].

Communication-efficient implementation of OT_1^n can be viewed as a single-server PIR protocols with an additional guarantee that only one out of n secrets is learned by the user and the remaining $n-1$ remain hidden.

In [68], it is noted that their PIR protocol can also be made into an OT_1^n protocol, showing the first OT_1^n protocol with sublinear communication complexity. Naor and Pinkas [83] have subsequently shown how to turn any PIR protocol into an OT_1^n protocol with one invocation of a single-databased PIR protocol and logarithmic number of invocations of OT_1^2 protocol. With reference to Section 1.5.2, an important feature of Naor-Pinkas OT_1^n protocol is that for A to obtain the value of the desired X_I, she does not need all of $Y_1, Y_2, \cdots, Y_n$, but only Y_I. Therefore, if instead of getting $Y_1, Y_2, \cdots, Y_n$ from B, A can perform a PIR reading of $Y_1, Y_2, \cdots, Y_n$ with B, then A can get sufficient information without giving B any information about the value she is interested in. The added communication complexity to the PIR protocol is the $\log n$ invocations of the OT_1^2 protocol. The evaluation of the pseudo-random function F_K do not add to communication complexity. In this way, one can transfer any PIR protocol to OT_1^n protocol.

DiCrescenzo, Malkin and Ostrovsky [33] have showed that any OT protocol can be constructed entirely based on invocations of a PIR protocol; in other words, any single-database PIR protocol implies an OT protocol. That is, given any computational PIR protocol that is secure for the receiver, one can construct an OT_1^2 protocol. This method assumes that both parties are honest (but curious). Under this assumption, both the sender security and receiver security are maintained. By definition of the PIR protocol, the sender can obtain no information about the indices chosen by the receiver, and hence cannot distinguish which sequence is real and which sequence is artificial. If we assume that the parties can deviate from the protocol, then we can apply a transformation to account for the dishonesty. The focus of the transformation is the malicious receiver, since the sender cannot learn anything during the executions of the PIR protocol. The transformation consists of both the sender and receiver agreeing to a commitment before the execution of the protocol, and proving in zero-knowledge that it is correctly formed. This prevents the receiver from learning any more than allowed since once the commitment has been set, it cannot be changed for the duration of the protocol.

1.7 CONCLUSION

In this chapter, we have given a survey of single-database private information retrieval (PIR) and oblivious transfer (OT), including the security models for PIR and OT, and some classic PIR and OT protocols. In addition, we show the relationship between PIR an OT protocols.

There exist many nice constructions for PIR and OT protocols. For example, the PIR protocol based on the Φ-hiding assumption given by Cachin, Micali and Stadler [18], the PIR protocol based on trapdoor permutation given by Kushilevitz and Ostrovsky [69], the simulatable adaptive OT protocol given by Camenisch, Neven, and shelat [20], the OT protocol with access control given by Camenisch, Dubovitskaya, and Neven [19], the simulatable OT protocol based on identity-based encryption given by Green and Hohenberger [54], the practical adaptive OT protocol from simple assumptions given by Green and Hohenberger [55], the efficient, fully simulatable OT protocol given by Lindell [70], the simple adaptive OT protocol without random oracle given by Kurosawa and Nojima [67], etc. We have not listed all of them in the chapter. We refer to reader to [19, 20, 54, 55, 67, 70] for details about such constructions.

More recently, Mayberry, Blass and Chan [76] proposed a PIR protocol (PIRMAP), particularly suited to MapReduce, a widely used cloud computing paradigm. PIRMAP focuses especially on the retrieval of large files from the cloud and allow for optimal parallel computation during the "Map" phase of MapReduce, and homomorphic aggregation in the "Reduce" phase. PIRMAP has been implemented and tested in Amazon's public cloud with database sizes of up to 1 TByte. The evaluation shows that non-trivial PIR such as PIRMAP can be more than one order of magnitude cheaper and faster than trivial PIR in the real world.

CHAPTER 2

FHE-Based Private Information Retrieval

2.1 INTRODUCTION

Current single-database PIR protocols provide almost optimal communication cost, but require the database to use an enormous amount of computational power.

In 2007, Aguilar-Melchor and Gaborit [1, 2] introduced a lattice-based, computationally efficient PIR protocol, in which the computational cost is a few thousand bit-operations per bit in the database. In this protocol, the user, who wants to retrieve an element of index i from a database composed of n elements, generates a query formed of n matrices $B_1, B_2, \cdots, B_n$, one for each database element. All matrices are soft disturbed matrices except B_i, which is a hard disturbed matrix. To generate soft and hard disturbed matrices, the user chooses two special parameters p and q and generates A and B, two random matrices over $\mathbb{Z}/p\mathbb{Z}$ such that A is invertible, and lets $M = [A|B]$. For each $j \in \{1, 2, \cdots, n\}$, the user compute a matrix $M_j = [A_j|B_j]$ by multiplying M by a random invertible matrix P_j. Next, the user generates a random scrambling matrix Δ as a $n \times n$ random diagonal matrix over $\mathbb{Z}/p\mathbb{Z}$. For each $j \in \{1, 2, \cdots, n\} - \{i\}$, the user generates a soft noise matrix D_j, a $n \times n$ random matrix over $\{-1, 1\}$, and computes the soft disturbed matrix $M_j = [A_j|B_j + D_j\Delta]$. Then, the user generates D_i, the hard noise matrix, by generating a soft noise matrix and replacing each diagonal term by q and computes the hard disturbed matrix $M_i = [A_i|B_i + D_i\Delta]$.

The user sends the query formed of $B_1, B_2, \cdots, B_n$ to the database server which encodes the n elements to n matrices $A_1, A_2, \cdots, A_n$ and computes $R = (A_1, A_2, \cdots, A_n)(B_1, B_2, \cdots, B_N)^T$, and returns R to the user. At last, the user retrieves A_i from R. Using analytical and experimental techniques, Olumofin and Goldberg [84] analyzed the performance of the lattice-based PIR protocol in 2010 and reported that the end-to-end response time of the protocol is one to three orders of magnitude less than the trivial protocol for realistic computation power and network bandwidth.

In 2008, Aguilar-Melchor, Gaborit and Herranz [3] provided a solution for securely evaluating multivariate polynomials of degree d with additively homomorphic encryption scheme. This scheme, further improved in 2010, can be used in PIR which requires secure evaluation of low-degree multivariate polynomials with a large number of monomials. The basic idea is to build a compound ciphertext $\alpha \otimes \beta = (\alpha^{(1)}\beta, \alpha^{(2)}\beta, \cdots, \alpha^{(t)}\beta)$, given the encryptions $\alpha = \mathsf{E}(a, pk) = (\alpha^{(1)}, \alpha^{(2)}, \cdots, \alpha^{(t)})$ and $\beta = \mathsf{E}(b, pk)$, where $a, b \in \{0, 1\}$. To decrypt the compound ciphertext, one decrypts each coordinate at first and then reconstructs the inner ciphertext $\alpha = \sum_i 2^{i-1}\alpha^{(i)}$ and decrypts it again to ab. This allows one to evaluate degree 2 polynomials over encrypted data. The idea can be generalized by iterating the construction to evaluate polynomials of degree d securely, at the price of an expansion factor for the length of the ciphertext which is exponential in d.

Homomorphic encryption techniques are often very natural ways to construct a variety of privacy-preserving protocols. For example, the PIR protocol of Kushilevitz and Ostrovsky [68] is based on the Goldwasser-Micali homomorphic encryption E [53], in which $\mathsf{E}(b_1)\mathsf{E}(b_2) = \mathsf{E}(b_1 \oplus b_2)$ for any $b_1, b_2 \in \{0, 1\}$, while the PIR protocol of Chang [21] and Lipmaa [71] are based on the Damgard-Jurik homomorphic encryption E' [30], in which $\mathsf{E}'(m_1)\mathsf{E}'(m_2) = \mathsf{E}'(m_1 + m_2)$ for any $m_1, m_2 \in \mathbb{Z}_N$. A generic method to construct a single-database PIR from a homomorphic encryption scheme was given by Ostrovsky and Skeith in [87]. These underlying encryption schemes support homomorphic computation of only one operation (either addition or multiplication) on plaintexts.

In 2009, Gentry [41, 42, 43, 44] constructed the first fully homomorphic encryption (FHE) scheme using lattice-based cryptography. FHE supports homomorphic computation of two operations (both addition and multiplication) of plaintexts. In the same year, Dijk, Gentry, Halevi and Vaikuntanathan [34] presented the second FHE scheme, which uses many of the tools of Gentry's construction, but which does not require ideal lattices. The scheme is therefore conceptually simpler than Gentry's ideal lattice scheme, but has similar properties with regard to homomorphic operations and efficiency. In 2010, Smart and Vercauteren [100] presented a refinement of Gentry's scheme giving smaller key and ciphertext sizes. In 2011, Brakerski, Gentry and Vaikuntanathan [14, 15] proposed fully homomorphic encryption schemes based on the learning with error assumption.

Motivated by recent breakthrough in FHE, Yi, Kaosar, Paulet and Bertino proposed single-database PIR and PBR protocols from FHE [106]. In [41], Gentry briefly described a single-database PIR protocol with communication complexity $O(\gamma \log n)$, where γ is the size of the ciphertext. The basic idea is that the user, who wishes to retrieve the i-th bit from a database with n bits, sends the database server the encryption of the index i, and the server sends back the encryption of the i-th bit computed by fully homomorphic properties.

Yi et al. extend Gentry's basic idea to a PBR protocol, where the user, who wishes to retrieve the i-th block from a database with m blocks, sends the server the encryption of the index i, and the server sends back the encryption of the i-th block computed by fully homomorphic properties, as if the user sends the index i and the server returns the i-th block. It can be seen that this solution is conceptually simpler than any existing PBR protocols without FHE.

Based on the formal model for security of single-database PIR [18, 40], Yi et al. have shown that such PIR and PBR protocols from FHE provide privacy of the user as long as the underlying FHE scheme is semantically secure.

The performance of their protocols depends on the underlying FHE scheme. The user and the server need to exchange $O(\gamma \log n)$ bits in their PIR protocol, and $O(\gamma \log m + \gamma n/m)$ in their PBR protocol, where n is the size of the database, m is the number of blocks in the database, γ is the ciphertext size, and the base of the logarithm is 2.

So far, existing FHE schemes have not been practical. Yi et al. [106] gave a variant of Dijk et al.'s somewhat homomorphic encryption scheme, from which they construct a practical PBR protocol. In addition, they have implemented the practical PBR protocol for a database composed of 10,000 elements of size of 200kbits. Their experiment has shown that their PBR protocol is practical.

The rest of this chapter is as follows. Section 2 introduces the definitions of FHE and an example of FHE; Sections 3 and 4 describes generic and practical PIR and PBR protocols from FHE given by Yi et al. [106]; Sections 4 and 5 analyze security and performance of their protocols; conclusions are in the last section. The presentation in this chapter is partially based on [106].

2.2 FULLY HOMOMORPHIC ENCRYPTION

In this section, we introduce the concepts of FHE scheme and single-database PIR protocol.

2.2.1 FHE DEFINITION

Formally, a FHE scheme consists of five algorithms as follows.

(1) Key Generation (KG): The algorithm takes as input a security parameter k and outputs a public and private key pair (pk, sk), where pk is public, while sk is kept secret.

(2) Encryption (E): The algorithm takes as input a plaintext $m \in \{0, 1\}$ and the public key pk, and outputs a ciphertext c, denoted as $c = \mathsf{E}(m, pk)$.

(3) Decryption (D): The algorithm takes as input a ciphertext c and the private key sk, and outputs a plaintext $m \in \{0, 1\}$, denoted as $m = \mathsf{D}(c, sk)$.

(4) Homomorphic Addition (Add): The algorithm takes as input two ciphertexts $c_1 = \mathsf{E}(m_1, pk)$, $c_2 = \mathsf{E}(m_2, pk)$ and the public key pk, and outputs a ciphertext c, denoted as $c = \mathsf{Add}(c_1, c_2, pk) = c_1 \boxplus c_2$, such that

$$\mathsf{D}(c, sk) = m_1 \oplus m_2,$$

where $\oplus$ is the addition operation in the plaintext space while $\boxplus$ is the addition operation in the ciphertext space.

(5) Homomorphic Multiplication (Mult): The algorithm takes as input two ciphertexts $c_1 = \mathsf{E}(m_1, pk)$, $c_2 = \mathsf{E}(m_2, pk)$ and the public key, and outputs a ciphertext $c = \mathsf{Mult}(c_1, c_2, pk) = c_1 \boxtimes c_2$, such that

$$\mathsf{D}(c, sk) = m_1 \cdot m_2,$$

where $\cdot$ is the multiplication operation in the plaintext space while $\boxtimes$ is the multiplication operation in the ciphertext space.

A FHE scheme (KG,E,D,Add,Mult) is semantically secure if, given any public key pk, no probabilistic polynomial-time (PPT) adversary has success probability greater than ϵ to distinguish $\mathsf{E}(0, pk)$ and $\mathsf{E}(1, pk)$, where ϵ is negligible in k.

2.2.2 DGHV SOMEWHAT SCHEME

In this section, we instantiate the "somewhat" homomorphic encryption scheme proposed by Dijk, Gentry, Halevi and Vaikuntanathan [34], called DGHV somewhat scheme for brevity. The scheme does not require ideal lattices.

In [34], a symmetric homomorphic encryption scheme was proposed as follows.

1. KeyGen: The key is an odd integer, chosen from some interval $p \in [2^{\eta-1}, 2^{\eta})$, where η is the security parameter.

2. Encrypt(p, M): To encrypt a bit $M \in \{0, 1\}$, set the ciphertext as an integer $c = M + 2r + qp$, where the integers q, r are chosen at random in some other prescribed intervals, such that $2r$ is smaller than $p/2$ in absolute value.

3. Decrypt(p, c): Output $(c \ mod \ p) \ mod \ 2$.

Given two ciphertexts $c_1 = m_1 + 2r_1 + q_1 p$ and $c_2 = m_2 + 2r_2 + q_2 p$, we have

$$\begin{aligned} c_1 + c_2 &= (m_1 + m_2) + 2(r_1 + r_2) \\ &\quad +(q_1 + q_2)p, \end{aligned} \tag{2.1}$$

$$\begin{aligned} c_1 c_2 &= m_1 m_2 + 2(2r_1 r_2 + r_1 m_2 + m_1 r_2) \\ &\quad +(c_1 q_2 + q_1 c_2 + q_1 q_2 p)p \end{aligned} \tag{2.2}$$

Furthermore, $(c_1 + c_2 \ mod \ p) \ mod \ 2 = m_1 \oplus m_2$ and $(c_1 c_2 \ mod \ p) \ mod \ 2) = m_1 m_2$. Therefore, the symmetric encryption scheme supports both additional and multiplicative homomorphisms.

In [34], an asymmetric homomorphic encryption scheme was also proposed as follows.

(1) KeyGen(k): Takes a security parameter λ and determines a (convenient) parameter set $\rho = \lambda, \rho' = 2\lambda, \eta = \tilde{O}(\lambda^2), \gamma = \tilde{O}(\lambda^5), \tau = \gamma + \lambda$, where γ is the bit-length of the ciphertext, η is the bit-length of the secret key, ρ is the bit-length of the noise, τ is the number of integers in the public key. Chooses a random odd η-bit integer p from $(2\mathbb{Z} + 1) \cap (2^{\eta-1}, 2^{\eta})$ as the secret key sk. Randomly chooses $q_0, q_1, \cdots, q_\tau$ from $[1, 2^\gamma/p)$ subject to the condition that the largest q_i is odd and relabels $q_0, q_1, \cdots, q_\tau$ so that q_0 is the largest. Randomly chooses $r_1, \cdots, r_\tau$ from $\mathbb{Z} \cap (-2^\rho, 2^\rho)$ and sets $x_0 = q_0 p$ and $x_i = q_i p + r_i$. The public key is $pk = \langle x_0, x_1, \cdots, x_\tau \rangle$.

(2) $\mathsf{Encrypt}(pk, M)$: To encrypt $M \in \{0, 1\}$, chooses a random subset $S \subset \{1, 2, \cdots, \tau\}$ and a random integer r from $(-2^{\rho'}, 2^{\rho'})$ and outputs the ciphertext

$$c = \mathsf{E}(M, pk) = [M + 2r + 2\sum_{i \in S} x_i]_{x_0},$$

where $[z]_{x_0}$ stands for $z(mod\ x_0)$.

(3) $\mathsf{Decrypt}(sk, c)$: To decrypt c, outputs

$$M' = \mathsf{D}(c, sk) = (c\ mod\ p) mod\ 2.$$

(4) Homomorphic Addition (Add): Given two ciphertext $c_1 = \mathsf{E}(m_1, pk)$, $c_2 = \mathsf{E}(m_2, pk)$ and the public key pk, outputs a ciphertext

$$c = \mathsf{Add}(c_1, c_2, pk) = [\mathsf{E}(m_1) + \mathsf{E}(m_2)]_{x_0},$$

(5) Homomorphic Multiplication (Mult): Given two ciphertext $c_1 = \mathsf{E}(m_1, pk)$, $c_2 = \mathsf{E}(m_2, pk)$ and the public key pk, and outputs a ciphertext

$$c = \mathsf{Mult}(c_1, c_2, pk) = [\mathsf{E}(m_1)\mathsf{E}(m_2)]_{x_0}.$$

This asymmetric encryption scheme supports both additional and multiplicative homomorphisms, too.

The security of the DGHV somewhat scheme is based on the approximate-gcd problem, that is, for a randomly chosen η-bit odd integer p, given polynomially many samples in the form $qp + r$, where q is randomly chosen from $[1, 2^{\gamma}/p)$ and r is randomly chosen from $\mathbb{Z} \cap (2^{-\rho}, 2^{\rho})$, determine p.

The DGHV somewhat scheme is semantically secure if the approximate-gcd problem is hard. The choice of parameters in the DGHV somewhat scheme achieves at least 2^{λ} security against all of known attacks.

2.3 GENERIC SINGLE-DATABASE PIR FROM FHE

In this section, we present the response generation circuit [106], from which one can construct a generic single-database PIR protocol based on FHE and then extend it to a generic single-database PBR protocol.

2.3.1 RESPONSE GENERATION CIRCUIT

Without taking security into account, a response generation circuit can be described as follows.

Inputs: An index $i \in [1, n]$ and an n-bit database $DB = b_1 b_2 \cdots b_n$

Output: b_i

Response Generation Circuit:

(1) Write the index i in the binary representation, denoted as $i = \alpha_1\alpha_2\cdots\alpha_\ell$, where $\ell = \lceil \log n \rceil$.

(2) For each index $j \in [1, n]$, write j in the binary representation, denoted as $j = \beta_{j,1}\beta_{j,2}\cdots\beta_{j,\ell}$. Compute

$$\gamma_j = \prod_{t=1}^{\ell}(\alpha_t \oplus \beta_{j,t} \oplus 1), \tag{2.3}$$

where $\oplus$ stands for XOR operation. If $j = i$, $\gamma_j = 1$ and 0 otherwise. This means only $\gamma_i = 1$.

(3) Output

$$R = \bigoplus_{b_j=1} \gamma_j. \tag{2.4}$$

If $b_i = 1$, then $\bigoplus_{b_j=1}\gamma_j = \gamma_i = 1$. If $b_i = 0$, then $\bigoplus_{b_j=1}\gamma_j = 0$. Therefore, $R = \bigoplus_{b_j=1}\gamma_j = b_i$.

The response generation circuit is implemented with two simple operations, $\oplus$ and $\cdot$, where $\cdot$ is equivalent to AND. It does not need IF-THEN statement.

The circuit requires the plain index i to generate the response R and thus cannot preserve user privacy. To do so, one can make use of the FHE technique to evaluate the response generation circuit with the encrypted index as input in next section.

2.3.2 GENERIC SINGLE-DATABASE PIR FROM FHE

The generic single-database PIR protocol is built on an FHE scheme (KG, E, D, Add, Mult) and consists of three algorithms (Query Generation QG, Response Generation RG, and Response Retrieval RR) [106].

At a high level, the user generates a public and private key pair (pk, sk) for the FHE scheme, sends the public key pk to the database server, but keeps the private key sk secret. Then the user chooses an index i, where $1 \leqslant i \leqslant n$, and encrypts i with the public key pk, and sends the ciphertext as a query to the database server. Based on the response generation circuit and homomorphic properties, the server computes an encryption of the i-th bit as a response based on the database, the query and the public key pk, and sends the response back. At the end, the user decrypts the response to obtain the i-th bit.

Assume that the user and the database server have agreed upon an FHE scheme (KG, E, D, Add, Mult) in advance, the single-database PIR can be described as follows.

Query Generation QG$(n, i, 1^k)$

Inputs: The size n of the database DB, an index $i \in [1, n]$, the key generation algorithm KG, the encryption algorithm E, and a security parameter k.

Outputs: A query $Q = (pk, \mathsf{E}(i, pk))$ and a secret $s = sk$, where (pk, sk) is a public and private key pair for the FHE scheme and $\mathsf{E}(i, pk)$ is the encryption of i with the public key pk.

Algorithm $\mathsf{QG}(n, i, 1^k)$:

(1) (The user) generates a public and private key pair (pk, sk) with the key generation algorithm (KG) and the security parameter k, i.e., $(pk, sk) = \mathsf{KG}(1^k)$.

(2) Assume that the binary representation of i is $\alpha_1\alpha_2 \cdots \alpha_\ell$, where $\alpha_i \in \{0, 1\}$ and $\ell = \lceil \log n \rceil$. (The user) encrypts each a_j with the public key pk, denoted as $\hat{\alpha_j} = \mathsf{E}(\alpha_i, pk)$. Let $\mathsf{E}(i, pk) = (\hat{\alpha_1}, \hat{\alpha_2}, \cdots, \hat{\alpha_\ell})$.

(3) Output the query $Q = (pk, \mathsf{E}(i, pk))$ and a secret $s = sk$.

Response Generation $\mathsf{RG}(DB, Q, 1^k)$

Inputs: An n-bit database $DB = b_1b_2 \cdots b_n$, a query $Q = (pk, \mathsf{E}(i, pk))$, E, Add, Mult, and a security parameter k.

Output: A response R.

Algorithm $\mathsf{RG}(DB, Q, 1^k)$:

(1) For each index $j \in [1, n]$, (the database server) writes j in the binary representation $\beta_{j,1}\beta_{j,2} \cdots \beta_{j,\ell}$. (The database server) encrypts each bit $\beta_{j,t}$ with the public key pk, denoted as $\hat{\beta_{j,t}} = \mathsf{E}(\beta_{j,t}, pk)$ for $1 \leqslant t \leqslant \ell$, and computes

$$\hat{\gamma_j} = \boxtimes_{t=1}^{\ell} (\hat{\alpha_t} \boxplus \hat{\beta_{j,t}} \boxplus \hat{1}), \tag{2.5}$$

where $\hat{1}$ is an encryption of 1.

(2) (The database server) computes

$$R = \boxplus_{b_j=1} \hat{\gamma_j}. \tag{2.6}$$

(3) Output the response R.

Response Retrieval $\mathsf{RR}((Q, s), R, 1^k)$

Inputs: $s = sk$, an output of $\mathsf{QG}(n, i, 1^k)$; R, an output of $\mathsf{RG}(DB, Q, 1^k)$, and the decryption algorithm D.

Output: A bit $b' = \mathsf{D}(R, sk)$.

Theorem 2.1 **(Correctness).** *The generic single-database PIR from FHE is correct for any security parameter k, any database DB with any size n, and any index $1 \leqslant i \leqslant n$.*

Proof. By comparing the response generation circuit and the response generation algorithm (RG), we can see that $\hat{\gamma_j}$ is an encryption of 1 when $j = i$ and an encryption of 0 otherwise, on the basis of fully homomorphic properties. Therefore, if $b_i = 1$, $R = \boxplus_{b_j=1}\hat{\gamma_j} = \hat{\gamma_i} = \hat{1}$, if $b_i = 0$, $R = \boxplus_{b_j=1}\hat{\gamma_j} = \hat{0}$. This means R is an encryption of b_i and thus $b' = \mathsf{D}(R, sk) = b_i$. □

2.3.3 GENERIC SINGLE-DATABASE PBR FROM FHE

Now, one can extend the single-database PIR from FHE to a single-database PBR from FHE, which also consists of three algorithms (QG, RG, RR) [106].

Assume that an n-bit database DB is equally partitioned into m blocks, denoted as $DB = B_1\|B_2\cdots\|B_m$, the single-database PBR is described as follows.

Query Generation $\mathsf{QG}(m, i, 1^k)$

Inputs: The number m of blocks in the database DB, an index $i \in [1, m]$, KG, E, and a security parameter k.

Outputs: A query $Q = (pk, \mathsf{E}(i, pk))$ and a secret $s = sk$, where (pk, sk) is a public and private key pair for the FHE scheme.

Algorithm $\mathsf{QG}(m, i, 1^k)$:

(1) (The user) generates a public and private key pair (pk, sk) with the key generation algorithm (KG) and the security parameter k, i.e., $(pk, sk) = \mathsf{KG}(1^k)$.

(2) Assume that the binary representation of i is $\alpha_1\alpha_2\cdots\alpha_\ell$, where $\alpha_i \in \{0, 1\}$ and $\ell = \lceil \log m \rceil$. (The user) encrypts each a_j with the public key pk, denoted as $\hat{\alpha_j} = \mathsf{E}(\alpha_i, pk)$. Let $\mathsf{E}(i, pk) = (\hat{\alpha_1}, \hat{\alpha_2}, \cdots, \hat{\alpha_\ell})$.

(3) Output the query $Q = (pk, \mathsf{E}(i, pk))$ and a secret $s = sk$.

Response Generation $\mathsf{RG}(DB, Q, 1^k)$

Inputs: An n-bit database $DB = B_1\|B_2\cdots\|B_m$, where $B_j = (b_{j,1}, b_{j,2}, \cdots, b_{j,L})$ and $L = n/m$, a query $Q = (pk, \mathsf{E}(i, pk))$, E, Add, Mult, and a security parameter k.

Output: A response R.

Algorithm $\mathsf{RG}(DB, Q, 1^k)$:

(1) For each index $j \in [1, m]$, (the database server) writes j in the binary representation $\beta_{j,1}\beta_{j,2}\cdots\beta_{j,\ell}$. (The database server) encrypts each bit $\beta_{j,t}$ with the public key pk, denoted as $\hat{\beta_{j,t}} = \mathsf{E}(\beta_{j,t}, pk)$ for $1 \leqslant t \leqslant \ell$, and computes

$$\hat{\gamma_j} = \boxtimes_{t=1}^{\ell}(\hat{\alpha_t} \boxplus \hat{\beta_{j,t}} \boxplus \hat{1}). \tag{2.7}$$

(2) For each $c \in [1, L]$, (the database server) computes

$$R_c = \boxplus_{b_{j,c}=1} \hat{\gamma}_j. \tag{2.8}$$

(3) Output the response

$$R = (R_1, R_2, \cdots, R_L).$$

Response Retrieval $\mathsf{RR}((Q, s), R)$

Inputs: $s = sk$, an output of $\mathsf{QG}(n, i, 1^k)$; R, an output of $\mathsf{RG}(DB, Q, 1^k)$, and D.

Output: A block $B' = (\mathsf{D}(R_1, sk), \mathsf{D}(R_2, sk), \cdots, \mathsf{D}(R_L, sk))$.

Theorem 2.2 (Correctness). *The generic single-database PBR from FHE is correct for any security parameter k, any database DB with any size n and any number m of blocks, and any index $1 \leqslant i \leqslant m$.*

Proof. The generic single-database PBR can be viewed as running L generic single-database PIR protocols in parallel. In each single-database PIR, the user retrieves the i-th bit from an m-bit database $DB_c = b_{1,c}b_{2,c} \cdots b_{m,c}$ for $1 \leqslant c \leqslant L$.

Based on Theorem 2.1, we know each of L single-database PIR protocol is correct, that is, $\mathsf{D}(R_c, sk) = b_{i,c}$ for $1 \leqslant c \leqslant L$. Therefore, we have $B' = (\mathsf{D}(R_1, sk), \mathsf{D}(R_2, sk), \cdots, \mathsf{D}(R_L, sk)) = B_i$. □

2.4 PRACTICAL SINGLE-DATABASE PIR FROM FHE

So far, existing fully homomorphic encryption schemes have not been practical for application in PIR. In this section, we present the variant of DGHV somewhat scheme for PBR and then the practical PBR protocol constructed from it [106].

2.4.1 A VARIANT OF DGHV SOMEWHAT SCHEME

A major difficulty in making the DGHV somewhat scheme practical is the size of the public keys. For the purpose of PIR and PBR, the database server does not need to perform any encryption operation except from some addition and multiplication operations of ciphertexts which require x_0 only. In addition, the user, who generates the private key p, is able to encrypt the index of the bit or block of interest directly by using the secret key p and the public key x_0. Therefore, the public keys $x_1, x_2, \cdots, x_\tau$ become redundant in PIR and PBR. In view of this, Yi et al. [106] introduced a variant of the DGHV somewhat scheme (V-DGHV) for PBR with a database of m blocks as follows.

(1) KeyGen(λ): The user takes a security parameter λ and determines a parameter set $\rho = \lambda, \eta = (\lambda + 3)\lceil \log m \rceil, \gamma = 5(\lambda + 3)\lceil \log m \rceil / 2$. Chooses a random odd η-bit integer p from $(2\mathbb{Z} + 1) \cap (2^{\eta-1}, 2^{\eta})$ as the secret key sk. Randomly chooses q_0 from $(2\mathbb{Z} + 1) \cap [1, 2^{\gamma}/p)$ and sets $x_0 = q_0 p$. The public key is $pk = x_0$.

(2) Encrypt(pk, M): To encrypt $M \in \{0, 1\}$, the user, who knows the secret key $sk = p$, randomly chooses q from $[1, 2^{\gamma}/p)$ and an integer r from $(-2^{\rho}, 2^{\rho})$ and outputs the ciphertext

$$c = \mathsf{E}(M, pk) = (M + 2 \cdot r + q \cdot p) \; mod \; x_0.$$

(3) Decrypt(sk, c): With the secret key p, the user decrypts a ciphertext as the DGHV somewhat scheme, that is,

$$M = \mathsf{D}(c, sk) = (c \; mod \; p) \; mod \; 2.$$

(4) Homomorphic Addition (Add): Using the public key x_0, the database server adds two ciphertexts c_1 and c_2 as the DGHV somewhat scheme, that is,

$$\mathsf{Add}(c_1, c_2) = (c_1 + c_2) \; mod \; x_0.$$

(5) Homomorphic Multiplication (Mult): Using the public key x_0, the database server multiplies two ciphertexts c_1 and c_2 as the DGHV somewhat scheme, that is,

$$\mathsf{Mult}(c_1, c_2) = (c_1 \cdot c_2) \; mod \; x_0.$$

Because the ciphertexts produced with p and x_0 are equivalent to those produced with the public keys $x_0, x_1, \cdots, x_{\tau}$, the variant of DGHV somewhat scheme can achieve at least 2^{λ} security against all of known attacks like in the DGHV somewhat scheme.

2.4.2 PRACTICAL SINGLE-DATABASE PBR FROM V-DGHV SCHEME

Assume that an n-bit database DB is equally partitioned into m blocks, denoted as $DB = B_1 \| B_2 \cdots \| B_m$, the practical single-database PBR from the variant of DGHV scheme is described as follows.

Query Generation QG$(m, i, 1^k)$

Inputs: The number m of blocks in the database DB, an index $i \in [1, m]$, KG, E, and a security parameter k.

Outputs: A query $Q = (x_0, \mathsf{E}(i, pk))$ and a secret $sk = p$, where (x_0, p) is a public and private key pair for the V-DGHV scheme.

Algorithm QG$(m, i, 1^k)$:

(1) (The user) generates a public and private key pair (x_0, p) with the key generation algorithm (KG) of the V-DGHV scheme and the security parameter k.

(2) Assume that the binary representation of i is $\alpha_1\alpha_2\cdots\alpha_\ell$, where $\alpha_i \in \{0,1\}$ and $\ell = \lceil \log m \rceil$. (The user) encrypts each a_j with the public key x_0, denoted as $\hat{\alpha_j} = \mathsf{E}(\alpha_j, x_0) = (\alpha_j + 2 \cdot r_j + q_j \cdot p)\ mod\ x_0$, where r_j and q_j are randomly chosen on the basis of V-DGHV scheme. Let $\mathsf{E}(i, x_0) = (\hat{\alpha_1}, \hat{\alpha_2}, \cdots, \hat{\alpha_\ell})$.

(3) Output the query $Q = (x_0, \mathsf{E}(i, x_0))$ and a secret $sk = p$.

Response Generation $\mathsf{RG}(DB, Q, 1^k)$

Inputs: An n-bit database $DB = B_1 \| B_2 \cdots \| B_m$, where $B_j = (b_{j,1}, b_{j,2}, \cdots, b_{j,L})$ and $L = n/m$, a query $Q = (x_0, \mathsf{E}(i, x_0))$, E, Add, Mult, and a security parameter k.

Output: A response R.

Algorithm $\mathsf{RG}(DB, Q, 1^k)$:

(1) For each index $j \in [1, m]$, (the database server) writes j in the binary representation $\beta_{j,1}\beta_{j,2}\cdots\beta_{j,\ell}$. (The database server) computes

$$\hat{\gamma_j} = \prod_{t=1}^{\ell} (\hat{\alpha_t} + (\beta_{j,t} \oplus 1))\ mod\ x_0 \tag{2.9}$$

(2) For each $c \in [1, L]$, (the database server) computes

$$R_c = \sum_{b_{j,c}=1} \hat{\gamma_j}\ mod\ x_0 \tag{2.10}$$

(3) Output the response

$$R = (R_1, R_2, \cdots, R_L).$$

Response Retrieval $\mathsf{RR}((Q, p), R)$

Inputs: $sk = p$, an output of $\mathsf{QG}(n, i, 1^k)$; R, an output of $\mathsf{RG}(DB, Q, 1^k)$, and D.

Output: A block $B' = ((R_1\ mod\ p)\ mod\ 2, (R_2\ mod\ p)\ mod\ 2, \cdots, (R_L\ mod\ p)\ mod\ 2)$.

Theorem 2.3 *The V-DGHV scheme can correctly evaluate the response generation circuit of the practical PBR protocol.*

Proof. Suppose that the size of the noise in $\prod_{t=1}^{s} c_i$ is $\mathcal{N}(s)$, where $c_t = (m_t + 2r_t + q_t p)\ mod\ x_0$ is a fresh ciphertext and $r_t \in (-2^\lambda, 2^\lambda)$. According to Eq. (2.2), the part of the noise in c_1c_2 is $2r_1r_2 + r_1m_2 + r_2m_1$ and

$$\mathcal{N}(2) \leqslant 2 \cdot 2^\lambda \cdot 2^\lambda + 2^\lambda + 2^\lambda < 2^{2\lambda+2}. \tag{2.11}$$

For any $s > 2$, we have

$$\begin{aligned} \mathcal{N}(s) &\leqslant 2 \cdot \mathcal{N}(s-1) \cdot 2^{\lambda} + \mathcal{N}(s-1) + 2^{\lambda} \\ &< 2^{s\lambda + 2(s-1)} = 2^{(\lambda+2)s-2}. \end{aligned} \tag{2.12}$$

Therefore, for each $1 \leqslant j \leqslant m$, the size of the noise in $\hat{\gamma_j} = \prod_{t=1}^{\ell}(\hat{\alpha_t} + (\beta_{j,t} \oplus 1)) \ mod \ x_0$ ($\ell = \lceil \log m \rceil$) is less than $2^{(\lambda+2)\lceil \log m \rceil - 2}$ and thus the size of the noise in $R_c = \boxplus_{b_{j,c}=1} \hat{\gamma_j}$ for each c is less than $2^{(\lambda+2)\lceil \log m \rceil - 2} m \leqslant 2^{(\lambda+3)\lceil \log m \rceil}/4$, which is less than $p/2$.

In view of it, the V-DGHV scheme can correctly decrypt R_c for any $1 \leqslant c \leqslant n/m$.

□

Based on the correctness of the generic PBR from FHE (Theorem 2.2), we can see that the practical PBR protocol is correct as well.

2.5 SECURITY ANALYSIS

Since the single-database PBR protocol is a combination of the single-database PIR protocol and the practical FHE-based PBR protocol is a special case of the generic FHE-based PBR protocol, only the security of the generic FHE-based PIR protocol needs to be analyzed.

Based on the formal definition of security for single-database PIR protocol given in Section 1.2, one can conclude

Theorem 2.4 *Assume that the underlying FHE scheme is semantically secure, then the generic single-database FHE-based PIR protocol is semantically secure.*

Proof. We denote by (KG, E, D, Add, Mult) the underlying FHE scheme. With reference to [97], suppose that there exists an adversary (a database server) $\mathcal{A}$ that can gain a non-negligible advantage ϵ in the semantic security game for the generic single-database PIR protocol. We prove that there exists an adversary $\mathcal{A}'$ (built on $\mathcal{A}$) who can gain a non-negligible advantage in breaking the semantic security of the underlying FHE scheme as follows.

The adversary $\mathcal{A}'$ initiates the semantic security game for the FHE scheme with some challenger $\mathcal{C}'$, which will send $\mathcal{A}'$ the public key pk for the challenge. For messages m_0 and m_1, we choose $m_0 = 0 \in \{0, 1\}$ and $m_1 = 1 \in \{0, 1\}$. After sending m_0, m_1 back to the challenger $\mathcal{C}'$, the adversary $\mathcal{A}'$ will receive $e_b = \mathsf{E}(m_b)$, an encryption of one of these two values. Next, $\mathcal{A}'$, playing a challenger $\mathcal{C}$, initiates the single-database PIR game with the adversary $\mathcal{A}$ with an n-bit database, who will give $\mathcal{A}'$ two different indices $1 \leqslant i, j \leqslant n$.

Let $x_0 = i$ and $x_1 = j$. The adversary $\mathcal{A}'$ picks a random bit q, and constructs a Q_q as follows: Assume that the binary expression of x_q is $(\alpha_{q,1}\alpha_{q,2} \cdots \alpha_{q,\ell})$ where $\ell = \log n$. The adversary $\mathcal{A}'$ constructs the encryption of x_q by replacing all zeros with $\hat{0}$ and all ones with $\hat{0} \boxplus e_b$. Note that $\hat{0}$ is the encryption of 0 with the public key pk and different random numbers are chosen in $\hat{0}$ for different bits. We denote the result as $Y_q = (\hat{y_{q,1}}, \hat{y_{q,2}}, \cdots, \hat{y_{q\ell}})$.

Now the adversary $\mathcal{A}'$ gives a query $Q_q = (pk, Y_q)$ to the adversary $\mathcal{A}$, who then returns a guess q'. With probability 1/2, e_b is the encryption of 0, and hence Y_q is the encryption of all zeros, $\hat{\gamma_z} = \boxtimes_{t=1}^{\ell}(\hat{y_{q,t}} \boxplus \hat{\beta_{z,t}} \boxplus \hat{1}) = \hat{0}$ for all $1 \leqslant z \leqslant n$, and $R = \boxplus_{b_z=1} \hat{\gamma_z} = \hat{0}$. In this event, $\mathcal{A}$'s guess is independent of q, and hence the probability $q' = q$ is 1/2.

However, with probability 1/2, $e_b = \hat{1}$, hence Y_q is the encryption of x_q, constructed exactly as in the QG algorithm, and hence in this case with probability $1/2 + \epsilon$, the adversary $\mathcal{A}$ will guess q correctly, as the behavior of $\mathcal{A}'$ was indistinguishable for an actual challenger $\mathcal{C}$. The adversary $\mathcal{A}'$ determines his guess b' as follows: If $\mathcal{A}$ guesses $q' = q$ correctly, then $\mathcal{A}'$ will set $b' = 1$, and otherwise $\mathcal{A}'$ will set $b' = 0$. Putting it all together, we can now compute the probability that the guess of $\mathcal{A}'$ is correct:

$$\Pr(b' = b) = \frac{1}{2}(\frac{1}{2}) + \frac{1}{2}(\frac{1}{2} + \epsilon) = \frac{1}{2} + \frac{\epsilon}{2}$$

Therefore, the adversary $\mathcal{A}'$ has obtained a non-negligible advantage in the semantic security game for the underlying FHE scheme, a contradiction to the assumption in the theorem. Thus, the generic PIR protocol is semantically secure according to the security definition.

□

2.6 PERFORMANCE ANALYSIS

The PIR protocol is a special case of the PBR protocol when each block contains a single bit. Yi. et al. [106] have analyzed the performance of the single-database PBR protocol and then compare it with some existing protocols.

2.6.1 THEORETIC PERFORMANCE ANALYSIS

In the generic single-database PBR from FHE, assume that the database DB has n bits, which are equally divided into m blocks, the user needs to encrypt $\log m$ bits and decrypt n/m ciphertexts, while the database server needs to perform about $m \log m$ Mult operations with reference to Eq. (2.7) and about $n/2$ Add operations in average with reference to Eq. (2.8). The user and the database server need to exchange the public key pk and $\log m + n/m$ ciphertexts. Assume that the ciphertext size is γ, then the communication complexity is $O(\gamma \log m + \gamma n/m)$ bits plus the public key size.

The generic single-database PBR protocol is built on a FHE scheme. So far, several FHE schemes have been proposed, such as [34, 41, 100, 101]. Recently, Gentry and Halevi implemented their lattice-based FHE scheme [45]. In order to evaluate all kinds of circuits, all existing FHE schemes are impractical. However, FHE schemes are usually constructed from simple and practical somewhat homomorphic encryption schemes, which are able to evaluate some simple circuits.

In the generic single-database PBR protocol, the degree of the boolean function corresponding to the response generation circuit evaluated by the database server is about $\log m$ only.

Therefore, it is possible for the PBR protocol to build on a somewhat homomorphic encryption scheme in appropriate setting.

In the practical single-database PBR protocol, the public key x_0 has the same size as a ciphertext, and the Add and Mult operations are modular addition and multiplication. Therefore, the total communication complexity is $O(\gamma \log m + \gamma n/m)$ bits and the computation complexity for the database server to generate a response is $O(m\gamma^2 \log m + n\gamma/2)$ bit operations.

2.6.2 EXPERIMENT

Assume that the database DB is equally partitioned into $m = 10000$ blocks, and the underlying encryption scheme is a variant of the DGHV somewhat homomorphic encryption scheme [34] with parameters $\lambda = 60, \eta = 882, \gamma = 2205$. In this setting, the somewhat encryption scheme is able to evaluate the response generation circuit of the practical PBR protocol without error and achieve the security level of 2^{60}. Both the ciphertext size and the public key size are 2205 bits. Therefore, the total communication complexities for the practical PBR are about $33075 + 2205n/10000$ bits. When $n > 42431$, the communication complexity of the practical PBR is less than the database size n. If the database server compresses the ciphertexts as in [34], where a compressed ciphertext has the same size as an RSA modulus, i.e., about 1000 bits, the PBR protocol can reduce the communication complexity significantly.

To generate the response R, the database server needs to compute $\hat{\gamma}_j = \prod_{t=1}^{\ell}[\hat{\alpha}_t + (\beta_{j,t} \oplus 1)]_{x_0}$ and $R_c = [\sum_{b_{j,c}=1} \hat{\gamma}_j]_{x_0}$, where $\ell = \log m, 1 \leqslant j \leqslant m, 1 \leqslant c \leqslant n/m$. The computation complexity is about 130000 modular multiplications and $n/2$ modular additions in average, where the modulus x_0 has 2205 bits.

In this setting, Yi et al. [106] have implemented the PBR protocol (without compressing ciphertexts) with GMP version 5.0.2 [51], a highly optimized library for arbitrary precision arithmetic. In their implementation, they choose the private and public key pair (p, x_0) as follows.

$$
\begin{aligned}
p = &172081910395086409292005763749997110305966 01\\
&29893779942568467253655521644657786345719504128\\
&38051033305541156961429645296757557163794012509\\
&14003744945293157980595942640451243898446460567\\
&72770258422144622675796928192080365842783838721\\
&17798711637935783321639095583031 51
\end{aligned}
$$

$$
\begin{aligned}
x_0 = &26995994051987058340696791927386621148530680\\
&22878576811588518529882283935651584401459488934 0\\
&87296688435128519763918588539827986380073047672 8\\
&50029906828623735772820856851345107599684815399 0\\
&68834844484560226015533052296762300373118602702 8\\
&53598835463598922565343114993041755364809007877 8\\
&84002779917880632443523307887651676495030462476 4
\end{aligned}
$$

4712582666952265396425644224023035423627257744 10
8393358820643779457378083375453207509677127662 83
1538651438382983571314220305630314179493707713 16
4888378922743877533890055820293982877136259481 18
0267865338901324979649878519587136203349942691 30
1338687145970091849018350119450266186755514760 60
70523977230371667356941297787012675390603483

On an Intel(R) Core(TM)2 Duo CPU E4600 with clock speed of 2.40GHz, the encryption of one bit by $c = [M + 2r + qp]_{x_0}$ (including randomly generating r and q) takes about 0.00001 seconds, and the modular addition and multiplication of two ciphertexts take about 0.000001 seconds and 0.00006 seconds, respectively. The addition of two ciphertext without modulo x_0 takes about 0.0000001 seconds. The total time for the user to generate a query Q is about 0.00015 second, the total time for the database server to generate a response R is about two minutes, when the database size is 2×10^9 bits (equally divided into 10000 blocks, each of which has 200kbits). The PBR protocol allows parallel computation. If the database server runs 20 processors in parallel, it takes about 6 seconds to generate a response. In addition, the total communication overhead is about $(15 + 200000) \times 2205$ bits. Over a line speed of 100Mbits per second, the transmission time is about 4.5 seconds, which is negligible in comparison with the computation time.

2.6.3 COMPARISON

In these single-database PBR protocols based on FHE, the user sends the encryption of the index of a block to the database server and then receives the encryption of the block. It can be seen that the solution is conceptually simpler than existing PIR and PBR protocols.

In the PIR and PBR protocols [21, 40, 68, 71], the database server usually needs to compute about $n/2$ modular multiplications for a large modulus N in average. For example, the database server in the Gentry-Ramzan PBR protocol [40] needs to compute $g^e (mod\ N)$, where e has the same size as the database, i.e., n bits. Computing the modular exponentiation requires about $n/2$ multiplications modulo N in average. In the practical PBR protocol based on FHE, the database server needs to compute about $m \log m$ modular multiplications and $n/2$ modular additions. Based on the implementation of the practical FHE-based PBR protocol where $n = 2 \times 10^9$ and $m = 10^4$, it takes about two minutes for the database server to generate a response (without parallel computation). In the same setting, the database server in the PBR protocols [21, 40, 68, 71], needs about 17 hours to generate a response. In terms of computation complexity, the FHE-based practical PBR protocol is more efficient than those PBR protocols when the block in the database has a relatively large size.

The single-database PBR protocols built on an FHE scheme can encrypt only one bit. They encrypt a block of bits in the database bit by bit and therefore their communication complexity $O(\gamma \log m + \gamma n/m)$ is higher than $O(\log^2 n)$, the current best bound for communication complexity. With the deployment of 100 Gigabit Ethernet and the development of terabit Ethernet in the future, the transmission for a large amount of data over the Internet will take less and less time. In practice, the timing difference of transmitting $O(\gamma \log m + \gamma n/m)$ bits and $O(\log^2 n)$ bits over a high speed network is negligible when both transmissions take a few seconds, but the timing difference of generating a response is a few hours.

The performance comparison among KO [68], CMS [18], GR[40] and Yi et al. [106] protocols in the server side is shown in Table 2.1.

Table 2.1: Performance Comparison (Server)

Protocols	Comm. Complexity	Comp. Complexity
KO[68]	$O(\|D\|^{\epsilon})$	$O(\|D\|/2)$ Mult.
CMS[18]	$O(\log^8 \|D\|)$	$O(\|D\|/2)$ Multi.
GR[40]	$O(\log^2 \|D\|)$	$O(\|D\|/2)$ Multi.
Yi et al.[106]	$O(\gamma \log m + \gamma n/m)$	$O(\|D\|/2)$ Add.

In the lattice-based PIR protocol [2], suppose that a database has $n = 1000$ elements of size 2 MB and the user generates a query composed of $N \times 2N$ $(N = 50)$ matrices $B_1, B_2, \cdots, B_n$ over $GF(p)$ $(p = 2^{60} + 325)$ and sends it to the database server, which encodes the database to $L \times N$ $(L = 16 \cdot 2^6/3000)$ matrices $A_1, A_2, \cdots, A_n$, and computes the response $R = (A_1, A_2, \cdots, A_n)(B_1, B_2, \cdots, B_n)^T$. The computation complexity for generating a response is $O(10^{14})$ bit operations. For the same database, the experiment on a server with a T7700 Core 2 Duo processor in [2] showed that the response generation phases in Lipmaa [71], Gentry-Ramzan [40] and the lattice-based PIR [2] protocols take 33 hours, 17 hours, and 10 minutes, respectively. If the FHE-based practical PBR protocol runs over the same database, the computation complexity for the response generation is $O(10^{13})$ bit operations, one order of magnitude less than the latticed-based PIR protocol. Based on the same experimental results in [2], the FHE-based practical PBR takes about one minute to generate a response.

In the single-database practical PBR protocol based on FHE, the underlying FHE is the variant of DGHV somewhat scheme, whose security is based on the approximate-gcd problem (please refer to Section 2.2). Lipmaa [71] and Gentry-Ramzan [40] protocols are based on classic assumptions such as Φ-hiding or quadratic residuosity. The cryptographic assumption of the FHE-based protocol is weaker than those of Lipmaa [71] and Gentry-Ramzan [40] protocols. However, the FHE-based construction is much simpler.

The additively homomorphic encryption scheme with d-operand multiplications proposed by Aguilar-Melchor et al. [3] can be used to evaluate the multivariate polynomials (2.7) and (2.8) for encrypted data in the FHE-based PBR protocol. This scheme needs two chainable encryptions to combine two ciphertexts to one ciphertext and a series of chainable decryptions to decrypt a combined ciphertext. The variant of DGHV somewhat scheme needs only one modular operation to combine two ciphertext to one ciphertext and only one modular operation to decrypt a combined ciphertext. For the same efficiency, the PBR protocol built on the variant of DGHV somewhat scheme is much easier to be implemented than the PBR protocol built on Aguilar-Melchor et al.'s scheme [3].

2.7 CONCLUSION

In this chapter, we have presented generic single-database PIR and PBR protocols from FHE, and a practical single-database PBR protocol from a variant of DGHV scheme given by Yi et al. [106]. These protocols work as if the user sends the index of a bit or a block to the database server and then receives the bit or the block from the database server. Security analysis has shown that the generic single-database PIR is semantically secure if the underlying FHE scheme is semantically secure.

Yi et al. have implemented the practical PBR protocol based on a variant of the DGHV somewhat homomorphic encryption scheme for a database composed of 10,000 elements of size of 200kbits. On an Intel(R) Core(TM)2 Duo CPU E4600 with clock speed of 2.40GHz, their experiment has shown that their PBR protocol is practical.

Compared with existing PIR and PBR protocols, the PIR and PBR protocols built on FHE are conceptually simpler. The practical PBR protocol based FHE has lower computation complexity but higher communication complexity than existing PBR protocols. Overall, the practical PBR protocol based on FHE is more efficient than existing PBR protocols in terms of total protocol execution time when a high speed network is available.

Future work is expected to further improve efficiency of PIR and PBR protocols from variants of existing FHE schemes, such as [3, 14, 15].

CHAPTER 3

Private Data Warehouse Queries

3.1 INTRODUCTION

Data warehousing provides tools for business executives to systematically organize, understand, and use their data to make strategic decisions. A large number of organizations have found that data warehouses are valuable in today's competitive, fast-evolving world. In the last several years, many firms have spent millions of dollars in building enterprise-wide data warehouse. Many people feel that with competition mounting in every industry, data warehouse is the latest must-have marketing weapon—a way to keep customers by learning more about their needs [57].

A data warehouse is a subject-oriented, integrated, time-variant, and non-volatile collection of data in support of management's decision making process [60]:

- **Subject-oriented**: The data in the data warehouse is organized so that all the data elements relating to the same real-world event or object are linked together.
- **Integrated**: The data warehouse contains data from most or all of an organization's operational systems and these data are made consistent.
- **Time-variant**: The data warehouse keeps historical data to reflect how the data changed as time passed.
- **Non-volatile**: The data in the data warehouse is never over-written or deleted—once committed; the data is static, read-only, and retained for future reporting.

Data warehouses are built on a multidimensional data model. This model views data in the form of a data cube. A data cube, defined by dimensions and measures, allows data to be viewed in multiple dimensions. In general, dimensions are the entities with respect to which we want to keep records. For example, a sales data warehouse may keep records of the store's sales with respect to dimensions—time, location, and product. Measures are the quantities by which we want to analyze relationships between dimensions. Examples of measures for a sales data warehouse include the sales amount, the number of units sold, and the average sales amount. A data cube is multiple-dimensional. An example is the sales data organized with respect to three dimensions—time, products, and cities as shown in Figure 3.1.

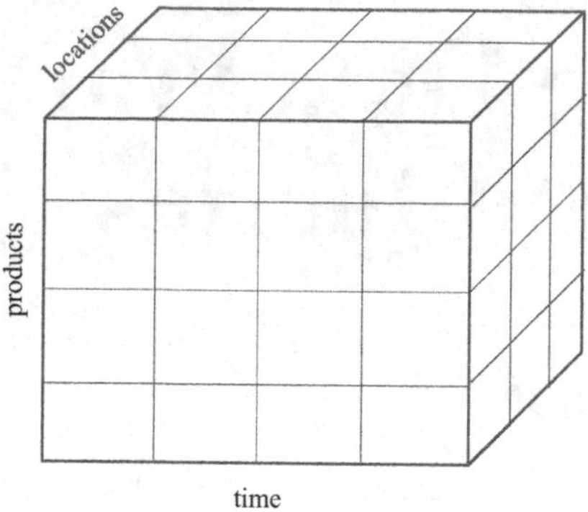

Figure 3.1: 3-D data cube.

In the multidimensional model, data is organized into multiple dimensions, where each dimension has multiple-levels of abstraction defined by a concept hierarchy. A concept hierarchy defines a sequence of mapping from a set of low-level concepts to high-level, more general concepts. The concept hierarchy for locations could be street, city, state, and country. This organization provides clients with the flexibility to view data from different perspectives. A number of online analytical processing (OLAP) operations exist to materialize these different views, supporting interactive querying and analysis of the data at hand. Typical OLAP operations include:

- **Roll-up**: Aggregation by climbing up a concept hierarchy. For example, roll-up from day to month along the time dimension in the sales data warehouse results in the sales amount, the number of units, and the average sales amount of a month in each cell.

- **Drill-down**: The reverse of roll-up. For example, drill-down from month to day along the time dimension in the sales data warehouse results in the sales amount, the number of units, and the average sales amount of a day in each cell.

- **Slice**: A selection on one dimension, resulting in a sub-cube. For example, slice on location dimension at a city in the sales data warehouse results in a sub-cube with two dimensions—product and time—where each cell has the sales amount, the number of units, and the average sales amount at the city.

- **Dice**: A selection on two or more dimensions, resulting in a sub-cube. For example, dice on location dimension in a state and time dimension in a year results in a sub-cube with three dimensions, where the location dimension contains all cities in the state and the time dimension contains all days in the year.

- **Pivot**: Rotating the data axes in view in order to provide an alternative presentation of the data. For example, pivot on a sub-cube with two dimensions time (x-axis) product (y-axis) results in a sub-cube with two dimension product (x-axis) and time (y-axis).

Queries to the data warehouse are based on a star-net model, which consists of radial lines emanating from a central point, where each line represents a concept hierarchy of a dimension. These represent the granularities available for use by OLAP operations such as drill-down and roll-up. A star-net query model for a sales data warehouse can be shown in Figure 3.2.

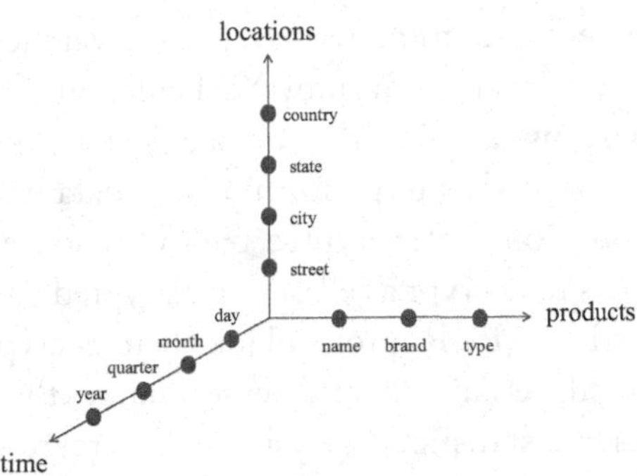

Figure 3.2: A star-net model for data warehouse query.

In order to query the data warehouse, a user usually first requests the server to perform OLAP operations and then sends back a cell. An important issue in this simple process is represented by the privacy of the user query as a user query may reveal to the server business sensitive information about the user. For example, for a stock exchange data warehouse, the user may be an investor, who queries the data warehouse for the trend of a certain stock. He may wish to keep private the identity of the stock he is interested in. For a pharmaceutical data warehouse, the user may be a laboratory, which would like to keep private the active principles it wants to use. To protect his privacy, the user accessing a data warehouse may therefore want to perform OLAP operations and retrieve a cell without revealing any information about which cell he is interested in.

A trivial solution to the above private data warehouse query problem is for the user to download the entire data warehouse and then locally perform OLAP operations and retrieve the cell of interest. This solution is not suitable if the owner of the data warehouse wishes to make profit through data warehouse services (for example, a health care data warehouse). Usually, the user is interested in only a part of the data warehouse. Purchasing the entire data warehouse may not be an economic way to the user.

Private Information Retrieval (PIR) protocols, such as [18, 24, 40, 68, 106], do not fully address the private data warehouse query problem. A PIR protocol allows a user to retrieve a record from a database without the owner of that database being able to determine which record was selected with communication cost less than the database size. By using PIR, a user can retrieve a cell (a record) from a data warehouse (a database) without revealing any information about which cell is retrieved. However, the user cannot hide his OLAP operations to the server when he requests the server to perform the operations. These operations may reveal the user's interest. For example, when the user requests the server to perform a slice operation with respect to a location, the server can learn the user's interest in the location. It is a challenge to assure the user's privacy when performing OLAP operations.

In this chapter, we present a solution for private data warehouse queries on the basis of the Boneh-Goh-Nissim cryptosystem [13], given by Yi, Paulet and Bertino [107]. Their basic idea is to allow the data warehouse owner to encrypt its data warehouse and distribute the encrypted data warehouse to the user who wishes to perform private data warehouse queries. The user can perform any OLAP operations on the encrypted data warehouse locally without revealing his interest. When the user wishes to decrypt a cell of the encrypted data warehouse, the user and the server run a Private Cell Retrieval (PCR) protocol jointly to decrypt the cell without revealing to the server which cell is retrieved. Assume that the server charges the client per query, their solution allows the user to perform some statistical analysis, such as regression and variance analysis, on the encrypted data warehouse with the lowest cost.

Unlike operational databases, data warehouses are non-volatile. The data in a data warehouse is never over-written or deleted—once committed; the data is static, read-only, and retained for future reporting. It is feasible to allow the data warehouse owner to distribute the encrypted data warehouse to potential users only once and later let the users download new added data online if any.

Yi et al.'s solution ensures both the server's security in the sense that the server, for billing purpose, releases to the user only a data per query, and the client's security in the sense that the client does not reveal any information about his queries to the server. Yi et al. have implemented their solution on an example of data warehouse, and experiments have shown that their solution is practical for private data warehouse queries.

The rest of the chapter is organized as follows. Boneh-Goh-Nissim cryptosystem is introduced in Section 2. We give the definition of Yi. et al.'s model and described their solution in Section 3. The security and performance analysis is carried out in Section 4. Experiment results are shown in Section 5. Conclusions are drawn in the last section. The presentation in this chapter is partially based on [107].

3.2 BONEH-GOH-NISSIM CRYPTOSYSTEM

We introduce the Boneh-Goh-Nissim cryptosystem [13] in this section.

3.2.1 BILINEAR GROUP

We use the following notations:

1. $\mathbb{G}$ and $\mathbb{G}_1$ are two (multiplicative) cyclic groups of finite order N.

2. g is a generator of $\mathbb{G}$.

3. e is a bilinear map $e : \mathbb{G} \times \mathbb{G} \rightarrow \mathbb{G}_1$. In other words, for all $u, v \in \mathbb{G}$ and $a, b \in \mathbb{Z}$, we have $e(u^a, v^b) = e(u, v)^{ab}$. We also require that $e(g, g)$ is a generator of $\mathbb{G}_1$.

   We say that $\mathbb{G}$ is a bilinear group if a group $\mathbb{G}_1$ and a bilinear map as above exist.

3.2.2 BONEH-GOH-NISSIM ENCRYPTION SCHEME

The Boneh-Goh-Nissim encryption scheme, BGN scheme by brevity, resembles the Paillier [90] and the Okamoto-Uchiyama [85] encryption schemes. The three algorithms making up the scheme are described as follows:

Key Generation $KeyGen(k)$
Given a secure parameter $k \in \mathbb{Z}^+$, run $KeyGen(k)$ to obtain a tuple $(q_1, q_2, \mathbb{G}, \mathbb{G}_1, e)$, where q_1 and q_2 are two distinct primes and the order of both $\mathbb{G}$ and $\mathbb{G}_1$ is $N = q_1 q_2$. Pick up two random generators g, u from $\mathbb{G}$ and set $h = u^{q_2}$. Then h is a random generator of the subgroup of $\mathbb{G}$ of order q_1. The public key is $PK = \{N, \mathbb{G}, \mathbb{G}_1, e, g, h\}$. The private key $SK = q_1$.

Encryption $Encrypt(m, PK)$
Assume the message space consists of integers in the set $\{0, 1, \cdots, T\}$ with $T < q_2$. We encrypt bits in which case $T = 1$. To encrypt a message m using the public key PK, pick a random r from $\{1, 2, \cdots, N\}$ and compute

$$C = g^m h^r \in \mathbb{G} \tag{3.1}$$

Output C as the ciphertext.

Decryption $Decrypt(C, SK)$
To decrypt a ciphertext C using the private key $SK = q_1$, observe that

$$C^{q_1} = (g^m h^r)^{q_1} = (g^{q_1})^m$$

To recover the message m, it suffices to compute the discrete logarithm of C^{q_1} to the base g^{q_1}. Since $0 \leqslant m \leqslant T$, this takes expected time $O(\sqrt{T})$ using Polland's lambda method [77].

3.2.3 HOMOMORPHIC PROPERTIES

The BGN scheme is clearly additively homomorphic. Let $PK = \{N, \mathbb{G}, \mathbb{G}_1, e, g, h\}$ be a public key. Given two ciphertexts $C_1, C_2 \in \mathbb{G}$ of messages $m_1, m_2 \in \{0, 1, \cdots, T\}$ respectively, anyone can create a uniformly distributed encryption of $m_1 + m_2 (mod\ N)$ by computing the product $C = C_1 C_2 h^r$ for a random r in $\{1, 2, \cdots, N-1\}$.

More importantly, anyone can multiply two encrypted messages once using the bilinear map. Let $g_1 = e(g, g)$ and $h_1 = e(g, h)$, then g_1 is of order N and h_1 is of order q_1. There is some (unknown) $\alpha \in \mathbb{Z}$ such that $h = g^{\alpha q_2}$. Suppose that we are given two ciphertexts $C_1 = g^{m_1} h^{r_1} \in \mathbb{G}$ and $C_2 = g^{m_2} h^{r_2} \in \mathbb{G}$. To build an encryption of the product $m_1 m_2 (mod\ N)$, (1) pick a random $r \in \mathbb{Z}_N$, and (2) let $C = e(C_1, C_2) h_1^r \in \mathbb{G}_1$. Then

$$\begin{aligned} C &= e(C_1, C_2) h_1^r \\ &= e(g^{m_1} h^{r_1}, g^{m_2} h^{r_2}) h_1^r \\ &= e(g^{m_1 + \alpha q_2 r_1}, g^{m_2 + \alpha q_2 r_2}) h_1^r \\ &= e(g, g)^{(m_1 + \alpha q_2 r_1)(m_2 + \alpha q_2 r_2)} h_1^r \\ &= e(g, g)^{m_1 m_2 + \alpha q_2 (m_1 r_2 + m_2 r_1 + \alpha q_2 r_1 r_2)} h_1^r \\ &= e(g, g)^{m_1 m_2} h_1^{r + m_1 r_2 + m_2 r_1 + \alpha q_2 r_1 r_2} \end{aligned}$$

where $r + m_1 r_2 + m_2 r_1 + \alpha q_2 r_1 r_2$ is distributed uniformly in $\mathbb{Z}_N$. Thus C is a uniformly distributed encryption of $m_1 m_2 (mod\ N)$, but in $\mathbb{G}_1$ rather than $\mathbb{G}$. We note that the BGN scheme is still additively homomorphic in $\mathbb{G}_1$.

3.3 PRIVATE DATA WAREHOUSE QUERIES

3.3.1 MODEL

The model for private data warehouse queries was given in [107], where we consider a data cube D with n dimensions $y_1, y_2, \cdots y_n$ and m measures $x_1, x_2, \cdots, x_m$, denoted as

$$D = (x_1, x_2, \cdots, x_m)_{y_1, y_2, \cdots, y_n}.$$

We assume that the data cube is provided by a server S and used by clients. The server S wishes to make a profit by providing data warehouse services to clients. The clients wish to gain some knowledge from D through OLAP operations on D without revealing their interests to S.

First of all, on input a security parameter k, the server S generates its public/private key pair $\{PK, SK\}$, encrypts the data cube D into $E(D)$ with the public key PK, where the values of all measure attributes are encrypted, but the values of all dimension attributes are in plaintexts. The encrypted data cube $E(D)$ can then be released to clients.

A client C can either download the encrypted data cube $E(D)$ from the server's website or request the server to send a compact disc (or CD for short) of the encrypted data cube by post. It happens only once because the data warehouse is non-volatile. For new data added into the data cube, we allow the users to download it online. The client can then perform any OLAP operation on the encrypted data cube $E(D)$ locally.

Remark In many cases, the "client" is actually an organization that then has no problem in downloading and storing the encrypted data warehouse $E(D)$ and performing OLAP operations on $E(D)$.

In order to retrieve a cell from the data cube D after several OLAP operations on $E(D)$ (i.e., to decrypt a ciphertext C from the encrypted data cube $E(D)$ after several OLAP operations on $E(D)$), the server S and the client C runs a Private Cell Retrieval (PCR) protocol, composed of three algorithms as follows.

(1) Query Generation (QG): Takes as input the public key PK of the server S, the ciphertext C, which is an encryption of either a measure value or a function evaluation of several measure values, (the client) outputs a query Q and a secret s, denoted as $(Q, s) = \mathsf{QG}(C, PK)$.

(2) Response Generation (RG): Takes as input the query Q and the private key SK of the server S, (the server) outputs a response R, denoted as $R = \mathsf{RG}(Q, SK)$.

(3) Response Retrieval (RR): Takes as input the public key PK of the server S, the response R and the secret s of the client, (the client) outputs a plaintext x, denoted as $x = \mathsf{RR}(R, PK, s)$.

A PCR protocol can be illustrated as in Figure 3.3 and is correct if, for any security parameter k, for any ciphertext C, $Decrypt(C, SK) = \mathsf{RR}(R, PK, s)$ holds, where $(Q, s) = \mathsf{QG}(C, PK)$ and $R = \mathsf{RG}(Q, SK)$.

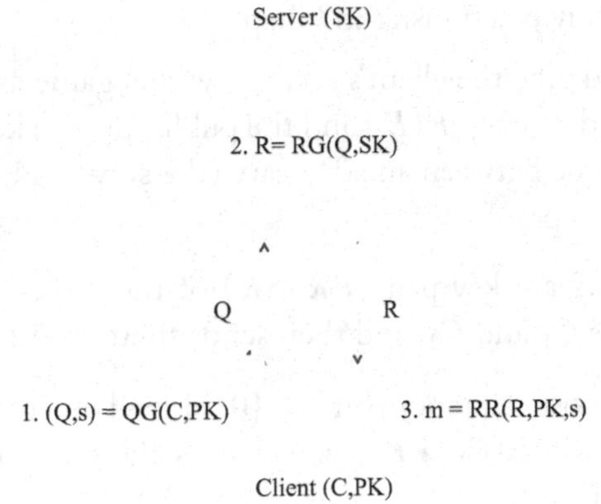

Figure 3.3: Private Cell Retrieval.

The security of the PCR protocol involves the server's security and the client's security. Intuitively, the server S wishes to release only one measure value to the client C each time when the client sends a query. Meanwhile, the client C does not wish to reveal to the server which cell is retrieved.

Formally, the server's security can be defined with a game as follows.

Given a data cube D and the public key PK of the server, consider the following game between an adversary (the client) $\mathcal{A}$, and a challenger $\mathcal{C}$. The game consists of the following steps:

(1) Given the public key PK of the server, the adversary $\mathcal{A}$ chooses two different values m_1, m_2 of two measure attributes and sends them to $\mathcal{C}$.

(2) The challenger $\mathcal{C}$ chooses a random bit $b \in \{0, 1\}$, and encrypts m_b to obtain $C_b = Encrypt(m_b, PK)$, and then sends C_b back to $\mathcal{A}$.

(3) The adversary $\mathcal{A}$ can experiment with the code of C_b in an arbitrary non-black-box way, and finally outputs $b' \in \{0, 1\}$.

The adversary wins the game if $b' = b$ and loses otherwise. We define the adversary $\mathcal{A}$'s advantage in this game to be

$$\mathsf{Adv}_{\mathcal{A}}(k) = |\mathsf{Pr}(b' = b) - 1/2|.$$

Definition 3.1 (Server's Security Definition). In a PCR protocol, the data warehouse server has semantic security if for any probabilistic polynomial time (PPT) adversary $\mathcal{A}$, we have that $\mathsf{Adv}_{\mathcal{A}}(k)$ is a negligible function, where the probability is taken over coin tosses of the challenger and the adversary.

Remark. Server's security ensures that the client cannot decrypt any ciphertext in the encrypted data cube $E(D)$ without the help of the server. The above definition for server's security is different from the definition for oblivious transfer in Chapter 1.

Next, we formally define the client's security with a game as follows.

Give an encrypted data cube $E(D)$ and the public/private key pair (PK, SK) of the server, consider the following game between an adversary (the server) $\mathcal{A}$, and a challenger $\mathcal{C}$. The game consists of the following steps:

(1) Given the public/private key pair (PK, SK) of the server, the adversary $\mathcal{A}$ chooses two different ciphertexts C_1 and C_2, and then sends them to the challenger $\mathcal{C}$.

(2) The challenger $\mathcal{C}$ chooses a random bit $b \in \{0, 1\}$, and executes the Query Generation (QG) to obtain $(Q_b, s_b) = \mathsf{QG}(C_b, PK)$, where s_b is the secret of the challenger $\mathcal{C}$, and then sends Q_b back to $\mathcal{A}$.

(3) The adversary $\mathcal{A}$ can experiment with the code of Q_b in an arbitrary non-black-box way, and finally outputs $b' \in \{0, 1\}$.

The adversary wins the game if $b' = b$ and loses otherwise. We define the adversary $\mathcal{A}$'s advantage in this game to be

$$\mathsf{Adv}_{\mathcal{A}}(k) = |\mathsf{Pr}(b' = b) - 1/2|.$$

Definition 3.2 (Client's Security Definition). In a PCR protocol, the client has semantic security if for any probabilistic polynomial time (PPT) adversary $\mathcal{A}$, we have that $\mathsf{Adv}_{\mathcal{A}}(k)$ is a negligible function, where the probability is taken over coin tosses of the challenger and the adversary.

Remark. Client's security ensures that the server cannot tell what information the client has retrieved from the data cube $E(D)$. The above definition for client's security is the same as the definition for PIR in Chapter 1.

3.3.2 PRIVATE CELL RETRIEVAL

Based on the model, we present the construction of the PCR protocol, proposed in [107], which allows the client to retrieve a measure value in a cell without revealing the measure and cell attributes to the server.

Their protocol is built on the BGN homomorphic encryption scheme [13] (please refer to Section 3.2). The data server S generates and publishes its public key $PK = \{N, \mathbb{G}, \mathbb{G}_1, e, g, h_1, e(g,g)^{q_1}\}$, and keeps its private key $SK = \{q_1\}$ secret.

Remark: Slightly different from the BGN scheme, Yi et al. replaced h with h_1 in the public key (please refer to Section 3.2) and include $e(g,g)^{q_1}$ as a public parameter. It does not affect the security of the BGN scheme because the discrete logarithm problem of determining the private key q_1 from $e(g,g)^{q_1}$ is hard, where q_1 is large prime. They publish $e(g,g)^{q_1}$ so that the client C can obtain the decryption privately.

Before releasing the data cube to clients, the data warehouse server S runs the Initialization algorithm to encrypt the data cube D to $E(D)$, as described in Algorithm 3.1.

Algorithm 3.1 Initialization (Server)

Input: $D = (x_1, x_2, \cdots, x_m)_{y_1, y_2, \cdots, y_n}, PK$
Output: $E(D) = (E(x_1), E(x_2), \cdots, E(x_m))_{y_1, y_2, \cdots, y_n}$
Let $E(D) = D$
For each measure value $x = (x_i)_{y_1, y_2, \cdots, y_n}$, where $1 \leqslant i \leqslant m$ and $(y_1, y_2, \cdots, y_n) \in DD$ (dimension domain), pick a random integer r from $\{1, 2, \cdots, N\}$, compute

$$z = Encrypt(x, PK) = g^x h^r$$

and replace $(x_i)_{y_1, y_2, \cdots, y_n}$ with z, denoted as $(E(x_i))_{y_1, y_2, \cdots, y_n}$. Note that the server knows h (please refer to Section 3.2) although PK does not include h.
return $E(D)$

After obtaining the encrypted data cube $E(D)$, if a client C wishes to retrieve a measure value in a cell, in other words, to decrypt a ciphertext C in a cell, the client C and the server S run the Private Cell Retrieval (PCR) protocol, composed of three algorithms, Query Generation

(QG), Response Generation (RG), and Response Retrieval (RR), as described in Algorithms 3.2-3.4.

Algorithm 3.2 Query Generation QG (Client)

Input: C, PK
Output: Q, s

Pick two random integers s, r from $\{1, 2, \cdots, N\}$
If $C \in \mathbb{G}$, compute

$$Q = e(C, g)e(g, g)^s h_1^r,$$

If $C \in \mathbb{G}_1$, compute

$$Q = Ce(g, g)^s h_1^r.$$

return (Q, s)

Algorithm 3.3 Response Generation RG (Server)

Input: $Q \in \mathbb{G}_1, SK = q_1$
Output: R

Compute

$$R = Q^{SK}.$$

return R

Algorithm 3.4 Response Retrieval RR (Client)

Input: R, PK, s
Output: m

Compute

$$R' = R/(e(g, g)^{q_1})^s$$

Compute

$$m = \log_{e(g,g)^{q_1}} R'$$

with Pollard's lambda method [77].
return m

Theorem 3.1 (Correctness). *The PCR protocol is correct. In other words, for any security parameter k, for any ciphertext C,*

$$Decrypt(C, SK) = \mathsf{RR}(R, PK, s)$$

holds, where $(Q, s) = \mathsf{QG}(C, PK)$ and $R = \mathsf{RG}(Q, SK)$.

Proof. In case of the ciphertext $C \in \mathbb{G}$, we assume that $C = g^{m'}h^{r'}$. With reference to Section 3.2, we have $Decrypt(C, SK) = m'$. In addition,

$$\begin{aligned} R &= \mathsf{RG}(Q, SK) = Q^{SK} \\ &= (e(C, g)e(g, g)^s h_1^r)^{q_1} \\ &= e(g^{m'}h^{r'}, g)^{q_1} e(g, g)^{q_1 s} h_1^{q_1 r} \\ &= e(g^{q_1 m'}h^{q_1 r'}, g)e(g, g)^{q_1 s} h_1^{q_1 r} \\ &= (e(g, g)^{q_1})^{m'} e(g, g)^{q_1 s} \end{aligned}$$

In case of the ciphertext $C \in \mathbb{G}_1$, we assume that $C = e(g, g)^{m'}h_1^{r'}$. With reference to Section 3.2, we have $Decrypt(C, SK) = m'$. In addition,

$$\begin{aligned} R &= \mathsf{RG}(Q, SK) = Q^{SK} \\ &= (Ce(g, g)^s h_1^r)^{q_1} \\ &= (e(g, g)^{q_1})^{m'} e(g, g)^{q_1 s} h_1^{q_1 (r+r')} \\ &= (e(g, g)^{q_1})^{m'} e(g, g)^{q_1 s} \end{aligned}$$

Therefore, $R' = R/e(g, g)^{q_1 s} = (e(g, g)^{q_1})^{m'}$ and we have $m = \log_{e(g,g)^{q_1}} R' = m'$, i.e., $Decrypt(C, SK) = \mathsf{RR}(R, PK, s)$. The theorem is proved. □

3.3.3 PRIVATE OLAP OPERATIONS

Typical OLAP operations include roll-up (performing aggregation by climbing up a concept hierarchy), drill-down (the reverse of roll-up), slice (performing a selection on one dimension, resulting in a sub-cube), dice (performing a selection on two or more dimensions, resulting in a sub-cube), and pivot (rotating the data axes in view in order to provide an alternative presentation of the data).

After obtaining the encrypted data cube $E(D)$, a client C can perform drill-down, slice, dice or pivot operation on $E(D)$ as he does on the original data cube D because the dimension values in $E(D)$ are in plain. It is obvious that the sub-cube obtained by slice, dice or pivot operation on the encrypted data cube $E(D)$ takes a form of encryption of the sub-cube obtained by the same operation on the original data cube D.

For a roll-up operation on $E(D)$, without loss of generality, Yi et al. consider summarizing a measure x_i along the j-th dimension from a concept $y_j \in \{a_1, a_2, ...\}$ to a higher concept $Y_j \in \{A_1, A_2, ...\}$, where for any a_s, there is A_t such that $a_s \in A_t$. They roll-up operation on $E(D)$ is described in Algorithm 3.5.

Algorithm 3.5 Roll-Up (Client)

Input: $E(D) = (E(x_1), E(x_2), \cdots, E(x_m))_{y_1,\cdots,y_j,\cdots,y_n}, PK, \{A_1, A_2, ...\}$
Output: $E(D)^* = (E(x_1), E(x_2), \cdots, E(x_m))_{y_1,\cdots,Y_j,\cdots,y_n}$

1: Let $E(D)^* = (E(0), E(0), \cdots, E(0))_{y_1,\cdots,Y_j,\cdots,y_n}$
2: For each encrypted measure value $x = (E(x_i))_{y_1,\cdots,y_j,\cdots,y_m}$ in $E(D)$, where $1 \leqslant i \leqslant m$ and $y_j \in \{a_1, a_2, \cdots\}$
3: If $y_j = a_s \in A_t$ and $X = (E(x_i))_{y_1,\cdots,Y_j,\cdots,y_n}$ in $E(D)^*$ where $Y_j = A_t$, let $Z = xX$ and replace X with Z in the cell $(y_1, \cdots, Y_j, \cdots, y_n)$ of $E(D)^*$.
4: **return** $E(D)^*$

Theorem 3.2 *In Algorithm 3.5, given* $1 \leqslant i \leqslant m$, *let*

$$X_{A_t} = E(x_i)_{(y_1,\cdots,Y_j,\cdots,y_n)}$$

where $Y_j = A_t$ *and* $x_{a_s} = (x_i)_{(y_1,\cdots,y_j,\cdots,y_n)}$ *where* $y_j = a_s$, *then* $Decrypt(X_{A_t}, SK) = \sum_{a_s \in A_t} x_{a_s}$.

Proof. According to Algorithm 3.5, we have

$$X_{A_t} = \prod_{a_s \in A_t} E(x_{a_s}).$$

Due to the homomorphic property of the BGN cryptosystem, we obtain

$$X_{A_t} = E(\sum_{a_s \in A_t} x_{a_s}).$$

Therefore,

$$Decrypt(X_{A_t}, SK) = \sum_{a_s \in A_t} x_{a_s}$$

The theorem is proved. □

Theorem 3.2 ensures that the roll-up operation on the encrypted data cube is correct.

3.3.4 PRIVATE STATISTICAL ANALYSIS

The data cube is encrypted by the BGN cryptosystem. As discussed in Section 3.2, the BGN cryptosystem has an additive homomorphism. In addition, the bilinear map allows for one multiplication on encrypted values. As a result, the BGN cryptosystem supports arbitrary additions and one multiplication (followed by arbitrary additions) on encrypted data. This property in turn allows the evaluation of multi-variate polynomials of total degree 2 on encrypted values.

In view of this, those statistical analyses on the data cube can be performed in private, which involves the evaluation of multi-variate polynomials of total degree 2 on encrypted values, e.g., regression and variance analysis.

Remark. Most practical homomorphic cryptosystems, such as RSA [96], ElGamal [36], Goldwasser-Micali [53], Damgard-Jurik [30], and Paillier [90] schemes, provide only one homomorphism, either addition, multiplication, or XOR. They cannot be used to evaluate multi-variate polynomials of total degree 2 on encrypted values. Some statistical analysis requires to compute multi-variate polynomials of total degree 2. Although fully homomorphic encryption techniques [34, 42, 100] can be used to evaluate multi-variate polynomials of any degree, the state-of-the-art is still impractical in applications because the ciphertext size and computation time increase sharply as one increases the security level. So far, the BGN cryptosystem [13] is the only practical encryption scheme which can evaluate multi-variate polynomials of total degree 2 on encrypted values. This is why Yi et al. choose the BGN cryptosystem as their underlying encryption scheme.

Let $f(x_1, x_2, \cdots, x_\ell)$ be a ℓ-variate polynomial of total degree 2. For a purpose of statistical analysis, a user wishes to compute $f(a_1, a_2, \cdots, a_\ell)$ in private, where $a_1, a_2, \cdots, a_\ell$ are measure values in the data cube D. Given the encrypted data cube $E(D)$, the user obtains the encryptions of $a_1, a_2, \cdots, a_\ell$, denoted as $E(a_1), E(a_2), \cdots, E(a_\ell)$ and runs Algorithm 3.6.

Algorithm 3.6 Private Evaluation (Client, Server)

Input: $f, E(a_1), E(a_2), \cdots, E(a_\ell), PK$
Output: $f(a_1, a_2, \cdots, a_\ell)$

1: Client computes $C = f(E(a_1), E(a_2), \cdots, E(a_\ell))$
2: Client and Server run Algorithms 2-4
3: Client obtains $m = RR(R, PK, s)$
4: **return** m

Theorem 3.3 *In Algorithm 3.6,* $m = f(a_1, a_2, \cdots, a_\ell)$.

Proof. Because the BGN cryptosystem allows the evaluation of multi-variate polynomials of total degree 2 on encrypted values and the degree of the function f is less than 2, we have that

$$C = f(E(a_1), E(a_2), \cdots, E(a_\ell)) = E(f(a_1, a_2, \cdots, a_\ell)).$$

Based on Theorem 1, we have that

$$m = Decrypt(C, SK) = f(a_1, a_2, \cdots, a_\ell).$$

The theorem is proved. □

Theorem 3.3 ensures that the private evaluation is correct.

3.4 SECURITY AND PERFORMANCE ANALYSIS

3.4.1 SECURITY ANALYSIS

In this section, we discuss the security of the PCR protocol in terms of the server's security and the client's security. We consider the server's security at first.

In the scenario of [107], the server wishes to make profit through data warehouse services. The business model is most likely that the server charges the client per query. In other word, the server reveals one measure value only in each client query. In order to prevent the client from knowing all data in the data warehouse without paying for queries, the server encrypts the data warehouse with the BGN cryptosystem [13], where the decryption key is known to the server only.

The security of the BGN cryptosystem is built on the subgroup decision problem: With reference to Section 3.2, let $k \in \mathbb{Z}^+$ and let $(q_1, q_2, \mathbb{G}, \mathbb{G}_1, e)$ be a tuple produced by $KeyGen(k)$ where $N = q_1 q_2$. Given $(N, \mathbb{G}, \mathbb{G}_1, e)$ and an element $x \in \mathbb{G}$, output 1 if the order of x is q_1 and output 0 otherwise; that is, without knowing the factorization of the group order N, decide if an element x is in a subgroup of $\mathbb{G}$.

We say that $KeyGen(k)$ satisfies the subgroup decision assumption if for any polynomial time algorithm $\mathcal{A}$, the advantage of $\mathcal{A}$ in solving the subgroup decision problem,

$$|Pr(\mathcal{A}(N, \mathbb{G}, \mathbb{G}_1, e, x) = 0) - Pr(\mathcal{A}(N, \mathbb{G}, \mathbb{G}_1, e, x) = 1)|,$$

is a negligible function in k.

In [13], it has been shown that the BGN scheme is semantically secure if $KeyGen(k)$ satisfies the subgroup decision assumption.

Theorem 3.4 *If $KeyGen(k)$ satisfies the subgroup decision assumption in the BGN scheme, the server in the PCR protocol has semantic security.*

Proof. Please refer to [13] for the proof that the BGN scheme has semantic security if $KeyGen(k)$ satisfies the subgroup decision assumption.

Slightly different from the BGN scheme, we replace h with h_1 in the public key and include $e(g, g)^{q_1}$ as a public parameter. Because $h_1 = e(g, h)$, the replacement does not affect the security of the BGN scheme. In addition, it is hard to determine q_1 from $e(g, g)^{q_1}$ because the discrete logarithm is hard, and $e(g, g)^{q_1}$ does not help to solve the subgroup decision problem at all, i.e., to decide if $x^{q_1} = 1$ given an element x. Therefore, the definition for the server's security is the same as the semantic security of the BGN scheme and the theorem is proved. □

Next, we discuss the client's security. Based on the definition of client's security, Yi et al. consider the following game:

(1) Given the public/private key pair (PK, SK) of the BGN cryptosystem, the adversary $\mathcal{A}$ chooses two different ciphertexts C_1 and C_2, and then sends them to the challenger C.

(2) The challenger $\mathcal{C}$ chooses a random bit $b \in \{0, 1\}$, and executes the Query Generation (QG) to obtain $(Q_b, s_b) = \mathsf{QG}(C_b, PK)$. According to Algorithm 2, if $C \in \mathbb{G}$,

$$Q_b = e(C_b, g)e(g, g)^{s_b} h_1^{r_b};$$

if $C \in \mathbb{G}_1$,

$$Q_b = C_b e(g, g)^{s_b} h_1^{r_b},$$

where s_b, r_b are randomly chosen from $\{1, 2, \cdots, N-1\}$ and known to the challenger $\mathcal{C}$. Then Q_b is sent back to $\mathcal{A}$.

(3) The adversary $\mathcal{A}$ can experiment with the code of Q_b in an arbitrary non-black-box way, and finally outputs $b' \in \{0, 1\}$.

Theorem 3.5 *The client in the PCR protocol has the semantic security.*

Proof. In Step 2 of the above game, the ciphertext C_b is blinded by random $e(g, g))^{s_b} h_1^{r_b}$. Without knowledge of random s_b, r_b, the adversary $\mathcal{A}$ cannot tell which ciphertext is blinded even if $\mathcal{A}$ can apply the decryption key SK on C_b in Step 3 to obtain $R_b = e(g, g)^{q_1 m_b} e(g, g)^{q_1 s_b}$ where $m_b = Decrypt(C_b, SK)$. In view of this, the adversary $\mathcal{A}$'s advantage in this game $(\mathsf{Adv}_{\mathcal{A}}(k) = |\mathsf{Pr}(b' = b) - 1/2|)$ is negligible. Therefore, the theorem is proved. □

Remark. In Algorithm 3.2, if $C \in \mathbb{G}$, the client generates the query Q in $\mathbb{G}$ by letting $Q = Cg^s h^r$ where s, r are randomly chosen from $\{1, 2, \cdots, N-1\}$ and sends the query Q to the server. But this may leak to the server the client's intention, such as whether the client is retrieving a cell or performing statistical analysis. Therefore, in order to keep the client's intention private, the client has to generate the query Q in $\mathbb{G}_1$ no matter whether $C \in \mathbb{G}$ or $C \in \mathbb{G}_1$ as in Algorithm 3.2.

3.4.2 PERFORMANCE ANALYSIS

The core of Yi et al.'s solution is their PCR protocol, composed of Query Generation, Response Generation, and Response Retrieval. Before the client and the server can run the PCR protocol, the server is required to encrypt the whole data warehouse D in Algorithm 3.1 and distribute it to the client. This initialization costs $O(|D|)$, computation complexity, and $O(|D|)$ communication complexity in the server, and $O(|D|)$ communication complexity in the client. This initialization happens only once. Then the client and the server can run the PCR protocol any number of times.

In the query generation (Algorithm 3.2) of the PCR protocol, the client generates a query (Q, s) with at most two exponentiations in $\mathbb{G}_1$ and one pairing, and sends a group element of $\mathbb{G}_1$ to the server.

In the response generation (Algorithm 3.3), the server receives a group member of $\mathbb{G}_1$ and generates a response R with one exponentiation in $\mathbb{G}_1$ and then replies a group element of $\mathbb{G}_1$ to the client.

In the response retrieval (Algorithm 3.4), after receiving a group element of $\mathbb{G}_1$, the main time of the client is spent on determining the discrete logarithm $m = \log_{e(g,g)^{q_1}} R'$ with Pollard's lambda method [77]. The computation complexity of Pollard's lambda method is $\sqrt{T}$ where T is the upbound of m.

Computation of exponentiations and pairings and communications of group elements of $\mathbb{G}_1$ can be very fast. Thus, the main running time of the PCR protocol is $O(\sqrt{T})$.

Next, we discuss the performance of private OLAP operations. The computation complexity for the client to perform drill-down, slice, dice, or pivot operation on the encrypted data cube is the same as that of the same operation on the original data cube. In Algorithm 3.5, assume that the domain for the dimension y_j includes λ different values, then the computation complexity of the roll-up operation is $O(\lambda)$ group multiplications, which can be done very quickly.

At last, we discuss the performance of the private statistical analysis. In Algorithm 3.6, to evaluate a ℓ-variate polynomial $f(x_1, x_2, \cdots, x_\ell)$ of total degree 2 at a point $(a_1, a_2, \cdots, a_\ell)$, the client and the server need jointly to run the PCR protocol once. For this evaluation, the client and the server can also run the PCR protocol ℓ times to retrieve $a_1, a_2, \cdots, a_\ell$ at first and then the client computes $f(a_1, a_2, \cdots, a_\ell)$ locally. Assume that the upbound of x_i (where $1 \leqslant i \leqslant \ell$) is T, then the upbound of $f(x_1, x_2, \cdots, x_\ell)$ is about T^2. In this case, the main running time of Algorithm 3.6 is about $O(T)$ while the main running time of ℓ PCR protocols is about $O(\ell\sqrt{T})$, usually less than $O(T)$. However, the client in Algorithm 3.6 needs to pay once while running ℓ PCR protocols needs to pay ℓ times. Therefore, the private statistical analysis Algorithm 3.6 has the lowest cost.

To balance the cost and the running time for private statistical analysis, the client may retrieve a part of $(a_1, a_2, \cdots, a_\ell)$ and then run Algorithm 3.6. The cost and running time are inversely proportional as shown in Figure 3.4.

Cost

Time

Figure 3.4: Cost and running time relation.

We can see that if the client wishes to perform statistical analysis on the data warehouse with less cost, he has to spend more time to get the result. If the client wishes to perform statistical analysis on the data warehouse with less time, he has to pay more to get the result.

So far, Yi et al.'s solution is the only one to provide private OLAP operations. In their solution, the PCR protocol is essentially a PIR protocol. Unlike existing PIR protocols, such as [18, 24, 40, 68, 106], the PCR protocol needs to communicate the encrypted data warehouse in the initialization to enable private OLAP operations. This happens only once. Without considering the initialization, the performance comparison of the PCR protocol with some single database PIR protocols are listed in Table 3.1.

Table 3.1: Performance Comparison

Protocols	Comm. Complexity	Comp. Complexity
KO[68]	$O(\|D\|^{\epsilon})$ any $\epsilon > 0$	client $O(\|D\|^{\epsilon})$ server $O(\|D\|/2)$
CMS[18]	$O(\log^8 \|D\|)$	client $O(\log \|D\|)$ server $O(\|D\|/2)$
GR[40] $(N = \prod_i {p_i}^{e_i})$	$O(\log^2 \|D\|)$	client $O(\sum_i e_i(\log N + \sqrt{p_i})[94])$ server $O(\|D\|/2)$
PCR [107]	$O(1)$	client $O(\sqrt{T})$ server $O(1)$

From Table 3.1, we can see that the PCR protocol is more efficient than other single database PIR protocols in terms of communication if we do not consider the initialization. In addition, only the solution supports private OLAP operations.

Compared with a centralized data warehouse which supports OLAP operations, Yi et al.'s solution has two advantages as follows:

- A centralized data warehouse cannot protect the privacy of OLAP operations required by the client even if PIR may be used to prevent the server from knowing the final cell retrieved by the client. Their solution can protect the privacy of both OLAP operations performed by the client and the final cell retrieved by the client.

- A centralized data warehouse is inefficient when multiple clients concurrently perform OLAP operations in the server and run PIR with the server. Their solution is distributed and the client can perform OLAP operations in his local computer and only run the efficient PCR with the server.

Remark. We should point out that Yi et al.'s solution may not be suitable for operational databases which need to update their data frequently. This will require their solution to run the initialization many times and as a result the performance of their solution would be worse than others. Their solution is in particular suitable for data warehouses where the data is non-volatile. In this scenario, their solution needs to run initialization only once.

3.5 EXPERIMENTAL EVALUATION

In order to evaluate the practicality of their solution, Yi et al. have done some experiments on the Oracle global data warehouse example,[1] which has four dimensions—Channel, ShipTo, Product and Time—and a units fact table storing three measures—units, sales, and cost. The date cube keeps 9 years sale history data and contains about 300,000 cells. Their experiment is executed on a desktop machine with an Intel Core i7-2600 processor, which has a clock speed of 3.40GHz, and 16GB of RAM, and they use SQL and C programming language.

First of all, they implemented the BGN cryptosystem [13], in which the elliptic curve structures $\mathbb{G}, \mathbb{G}_1$ and associated bilinear pairing e are provided by the Pairing Based Cryptography (PBC) library.[2] For the public/private key pair (PK, SK) where $PK = \{N, \mathbb{G}, \mathbb{G}_1, e, g, h_1, e(g, g)^{q_1}\}$, $N = q_1 q_2$, $h_1 = e(g, u^{q_2})$ and $SK = \{q_1\}$, we use the values in Table 3.2.

In their setting, they choose the two primes q_1 and q_2; each has roughly 512 bits in length, so that it is impossible to factorize N according to the current computing technology.

Based on the BGN cryptosystem, all measure values in the units fact table are encrypted. This initialization takes about five hours. The size of the original data cube is 45 Mbytes while the size of the encrypted data cube becomes 850 Mbytes.

Remark In practice, a data warehouse is a very sparse multi-dimensional data set. In this case, the size of the encrypted data cube can be significantly reduced because only the measures with values need to be encrypted. In addition, all possible measure values in the units fact table are less than 2^{32} and thus we can set $T = 2^{32}$.

Based on the encrypted data cube $E(D)$, four experiments have been done and can be described in what follows. The goal of these experiments is to determine the actual times required by various OLAP operations, from the most simple, that is, retrieving a single cell, to the most complex ones, such as performing regression analysis and variance analysis.

Experiment 1 (Private Cell Retrieval) Consider the ciphertext C in Table 3.2 which is the encrypted value of a cell the user wants to retrieve. To do so, the client generates a query $(Q, s) = QG(C, PK)$ with values of Q and s shown in Table 3.3, and sends Q to the server. The server generates a response $R = RG(Q, SK)$ as shown in Table 3.3 and turns R to the client.

The client computes $m = RR(R, PK, s)$ with Pollard's lambda method, where m =3346.

[1] http://www.oracle.com/technetwork/database/options/olap/global-11g-readme-082667.html
[2] http://crypto.stanford.edu/pbc/

Table 3.2: Setting *(Continues)*

Para.	Values
q_1	210754186407604102310925188159859071072187549 727704467965310206936564933603873461196303262 642786480951780132666506364093582465543068449 71313514949562360857
q_2	127707578650528883113295334590981718968728937 878725402284946055541062874329871667476514811 389292826651236287717409754447822015620351794 49188842497114643083
N	269149068365773261841824041671333984122651229 207631208954991210415522316622671277634208088 843014413860367743186861524577200017371584463 927286387273029973442850457450263045480185806 500527854730802543879971807379459036648210795 717878207455901709230864575970688020145718885 793966526448525040987835358478405002131
g	[38541583386952104107838945807346922321315262 760669641124899551348857051123127875141089007 714527824427443188616396621912530181137147121 870447696068628604002854494442009563963141580 756926191397532999397829406565934259561055970 554703419949372001563073197258958319877077753 2167417021560418316558441418907804321571267,9 480911976241807747934632097048398180200105998 822744599035552243464272721936069407066922848 681186534355607954535020561134603030182187722 681209428254633017341515467050549483142767178 688953392003318854120308972805480677016226334 643239789167325213173963299635951154235542201 237755220067092164079566743266180947221]

Table 3.2: *(Continued)* Setting

Para.	Values
u	[903551131917073490336503216710648192334117915544889480566310739571070321840570775402471569690537613027389581714771363666801446926117194008951547565593558019302228863503996052468020120803598903553764223842937528901665731800080427102901220212446495469181975802533045365192799501768179451748665538612420022361751 18,91 2344027756431780155354290188903324675733841740787763145254874581322292224322975064748193212958199166448817011496702247715615234597772446997187158932478383350155924174147669466800545683604965274044520824298815628219216171226207871262915839460264607006701663931343227843513463421038728027651110893806278679381 85]

The total running time of this cell retrieval operation performed using the PCR protocol is about 1.14 seconds.

Experiment 2 (Private OLAP operations) Given the encrypted data warehouse, the client performs a slice operation implemented by the following SQL query:

```
CREATE VIEW Catalogues AS
SELECT ShipTo, Product, Time, units, sales, cost
FROM units_fact_table
WHERE Channel="CAT"
```

where "CAT" stands for Catalogues. The resulting Catalogues view is a 3-dimension subcube, from which the client further performs a slice operation implemented by the following SQL query,

```
CREATE VIEW Mouse AS
SELECT ShipTo, Time, units, sales, cost
FROM Catalogues
WHERE Product="MOUSE"
```

The resulting Mouse view is a two dimension subcube, from which the client further performs a roll-up operation along the ShipTo dimension from customer to all (i.e., aggregating three

Table 3.3: Experiment 1 *(Continues)*

Para.	Values
C	[21522238738461525457804247592603098239082392 03878506375032543377436400538008015288946477 1 04609310042020669566447820111219825035223917 3 37694837993427441102174838120044518010260366 7 50286878977707670405079381650737148867828535 7 97412610493107345524676804397627280852017191 2 94849308280713904839422012086503989541407 51,3 80340106280280361166971065004263731384329052 6 20570465181906976966387484720834400991449131 4 49801779463794171461637672051372560196749661 8 67157419733110577542925180978314228286893492 3 40319445548694926378089375173160966987521386 5 342483211597115040375577714048719[illegible]2339756050 1504354625954115122449456036177479[illegible]03290]
Q	[13724215451079649073033016471841055766946184 45586472251020577475288959402872101858404177 8 96854266713418119533513610761378492509397018 9 67159511869340728666293760915343525950843551 6 12005164603596693925414411762670047028272760 8 62100050734287540337102832107731786513455380 5 22148345845485419757410148893399718161708 9,36 78919081062468266013395978603345351997138033 5 04048039841440057582215662983420645059406592 3 23520146846921471653717790338740952727991947 7 90692889660027263864396837601590636125040809 2 09267145140255660618030649309821130324402548 5 50050801173322523507003303048156495930878283 5 852683713705923144227097233354009986 6782]
s	18885767480755584952853279609689701392631490 3 57000947277935223162999316611277887677763040 2 39304488046105895135931577295341425438826579 9 01804344440181579264582451758128322831632170 1 04747913390842880631728084113645577766648340 1 75950963304312414823109662370652049584495612 0 643045136913607186633855095825607139394

Table 3.3: *(Continued)* Experiment 1

Para.	Values
R	[333243658719658408065982005629568505613085 99 6021403060183417149618139008163841174822239 46 3350827804843399577119545830922465717860990 78 3838226442733915537571065408876494730212311 57 5334829442110356526053767246765078747590433 52 2121033719436836883532917094531689184422662 50 8658836382194377646000106718592465709295906,6 7939810029376578830037729689851158604212740 50 7079462584901371078977358794020784614775284 07 9170144191312826454540092012650439111943565 56 804859002976782405306798948607 93............

measures—units, sales, and cost—for all customers), and then a roll-up operation along the time dimension from month to year (i.e., aggregating three measures—units, sales, and cost—from months into years), with Algorithm 5 implemented by the C programming language.

At last, the client obtains a subcube with only the Time dimension, which takes values in the set $\{0, 1, \cdots, 9\}$.

The total running time for the above sequential OLAP operations is under three minutes.

Remark The roll-up operation can be speeded up by parallel computation. For example, if we allocate the task for the roll-up operation to multiple computers and run five computers in parallel, the total running time for the above experiment can be reduced from three minutes to 36 seconds.

Experiment 3 (Private Regression Analysis) The sequence of the OLAP operations in Experiment 2 restricts and shapes the data warehouse so that it is ready for a regression analysis, by which the client would like to investigate the relationship between the number of sold mouse units and the time.

Consider the one dimension subcube that resulted from the sequential OLAP operations in Experiment 2, and assume that the units measure takes values $E(Y_1), E(Y_2), \cdots, E(Y_n)$ in years $X_1, X_2, \cdots, X_n$, respectively.

A simple regression analysis is to determine b_0 and b_1 in the linear equation $Y_i = b_0 + b_1 X_i$, where the formulas for the least squares estimates are

$$\begin{aligned} b_1 &= \frac{\sum_{i=1}^{n}(X_i - \overline{X})(Y_i - \overline{Y})}{\sum_{i=1}^{n}(X_i - \overline{X})^2} \\ b_0 &= \overline{Y} - b_1 \overline{X} \end{aligned}$$

where $\overline{X} = \frac{\sum_{i=1}^{n} X_i}{n}$ and $\overline{Y} = \frac{\sum_{i=1}^{n} Y_i}{n}$.

Given $X_1, X_2, \cdots, X_n$ and $E(Y_1), E(Y_2), \cdots, E(Y_n)$, to compute b_0, b_1, the client gets $\prod_{i=1}^{n} E(Y_i) = E(\sum_{i=1}^{n} Y_i)$ decrypted by the PCR protocol and then computes $\overline{X}$ and $\overline{Y}$. Next, let $[\overline{X}], [\overline{Y}]$ be the round results of $\overline{X}, \overline{Y}$ (note that the number of sold units is positive integer), and let

$$Z = \prod_{i=1}^{n} (E(Y_i)/E([\overline{Y}]))^{X_i - [\overline{X}]}.$$

Based on the homomorphic property of the BGN cryptosystem, we have that

$$\begin{aligned} Z &= \prod_{i=1}^{n} (E(Y_i - [\overline{Y}])^{X_i - [\overline{X}]} \\ &= \prod_{i=1}^{n} E((X_i - [\overline{X}])(Y_i - [\overline{Y}])) \\ &= E(\sum_{i=1}^{n} (X_i - [\overline{X}])(Y_i - [\overline{Y}])) \\ &= E(b_1 \sum_{i=1}^{n} (X_i - [\overline{X}])^2) \end{aligned}$$

Then the client gets Z decrypted by the PCR protocol and then computes $b_1 = Decrypt(Z, SK)/\sum_{i=1}^{n}(X_i - [\overline{X}])^2$ and $b_0 = \overline{Y} - b_1\overline{X}$.

By the above private regression analysis, we obtain the linear equation

$$Y = 9407.33 - 658.08X.$$

This result is very close to the actual linear equation $Y = 9407.67 - 658.08X$ obtained by performing the regression analysis on the plain data warehouse. In addition, the private regression analysis needs two decryptions only.

Remark. The difference between two linear equations is due to the rounding operation.

Experiment 4 (Private Variance Analysis) Consider the one dimension subcube that resulted from the sequential OLAP operations in Experiment 2, i.e., $X_1, X_2, \cdots, X_n$ (years) and $E(Y_1), E(Y_2), \cdots, E(Y_n)$ (encrypted units), and suppose that the client would like to compute the variance for units measure in private.

The variance v^2 can be computed as follows:

$$\begin{aligned} v^2 &= \frac{\sum_{i=1}^{n}(Y_i - \overline{Y})^2}{n} \\ &= \frac{\sum_{i=1}^{n}(nY_i - n\overline{Y})^2}{n^3} \\ &= \frac{\sum_{i=1}^{n}(nY_i - \sum_{j=1}^{n} Y_j)^2}{n^3} \end{aligned}$$

From $E(Y_1), E(Y_2), \cdots, E(Y_n)$, the client can obtain $E(nY_i - \sum_{j=1}^{n} Y_j) = E(Y_i)^n / \prod_{j=1}^{n} E(Y_j)$. Let

$$Z = e(E(nY_i - \sum_{j=1}^{n} Y_j), E(nY_i - \sum_{j=1}^{n} Y_j)),$$

where e denotes the pairing operation (please refer to Appendix). Based on the homomorphic property of the BGN cryptosystem, we have

$$\begin{aligned} Z &= \prod_{i=1}^{n} e(E(nY_i - \sum_{j=1}^{n} Y_j), E(nY_i - \sum_{j=1}^{n} Y_j)) \\ &= \prod_{i=1}^{n} \mathcal{E}((nY_i - \sum_{j=1}^{n} Y_j)^2) \\ &= \mathcal{E}(\sum_{i=1}^{n} (nY_i - \sum_{j=1}^{n} Y_j)^2) \end{aligned}$$

where $\mathcal{E}$ denotes the BGN encryption over $\mathbb{G}_1$ (please refer to Section 3.2).

Next, the client gets Z decrypted by the PCR protocol and computes $v^2 = Decrypt(Z, SK)/n^3$.

By the above private variance computation, the client obtains the variance $v^2 = 3212337.56$ for units measure with only one decryption. This result is the same as the actual variance by performing the variance analysis on the plain data warehouse.

Remark. If the underlying encryption scheme were the ElGamal scheme [36] or Paillier scheme [90] instead of the BGN scheme [13], the private variance analysis in Experiment 4 would have needed 9 decryptions instead of one decryption.

3.6 CONCLUSION

In this chapter, we have presented Yi et al.'s solution for private data warehouse queries. Such solution allows the client to perform OLAP operations, such as roll-up, drill-down, dice, slice, pivot, and then retrieve a cell from the resulted data warehouse without revealing to the server what operations are performed and what cell is retrieved. In particular, such solution allows the client to perform some statistical analysis on the data warehouse with the lowest cost if the server charges the client per query.

The described solution provides not only the client's security but also the server's security. Performance analysis and experiments have shown that their solution is practical for private data warehouse queries.

So far, such solution only allows the client to privately perform statistical analyses which can be algebraically expressed as a polynomial of degree at most 2 on the data warehouse, such as regression and variance analysis.

Future work is expected to extend Yi et al.'s solution so that the client can privately perform statistical analyses which cannot be algebraically expressed as a polynomial, such as min, max, and count.

CHAPTER 4

Privacy-Preserving Location-Based Queries

4.1 INTRODUCTION

A location-based service (LBS) is an information, entertainment, and utility service generally accessible by mobile devices such as mobile phones, GPS devices, pocket PCs, and operating through a mobile network. An LBS can offer many services to the users based on the geographical position of their mobile device. The services provided by an LBS are typically based on a point-of-interest database. By retrieving the Points Of Interest (POIs) from the database server, the user can get answers to various location based queries, which include but are not limited to: discovering the nearest ATM machine, gas station, hospital, or police station. In recent years there has been a dramatic increase in the number of mobile devices querying location servers for information about POIs. Among many challenging barriers to the wide deployment of such application, privacy assurance is a major issue. For instance, users may feel reluctant to disclose their locations to the LBS, because it may be possible for a location server to learn who is making a certain query by linking these locations with a residential phone book database, since users are likely to perform many queries from home.

The Location Server (LS), which offers some LBSs, spends its resources to compile information about various interesting POIs. Hence, it is expected that the LS would not disclose any information without fees. Therefore the LBS has to ensure that LS's data is not accessed by any unauthorized user. During the process of transmission the users should not be allowed to discover any information for which they have not paid. It is thus crucial that solutions be devised that address the privacy of the users issuing queries, but also prevent users from accessing content to which they do not have authorization.

The first solution to the problem was proposed by Beresford [9], in which the privacy of the user is maintained by constantly changing the user's name or pseudonym within some mix-zone. It can be shown that, due to the nature of the data being exchanged between the user and the server, the frequent changing of the user's name provides little protection for the user's privacy. A more recent investigation of the mix-zone approach has been applied to road networks [91]. They investigated the required number of users to satisfy the unlinkability property when there are repeated queries over an interval. This requires careful control of how many users are contained within the mix-zone, which is difficult to achieve in practice.

A complementary technique to the mix-zone approach is based on k-anonymity [12, 46, 56]. The concept of k-anonymity was introduced as a method for preserving privacy when releasing sensitive records [103]. This is achieved by generalization and suppression algorithms to ensure that a record could not be distinguished from $(k - 1)$ other records. The solutions for LBS use a trusted anonymizer to provide anonymity for the location data, such that the location data of a user cannot be distinguished from $(k - 1)$ other users.

An enhanced trusted anonymizer approach has also been proposed, which allows the users to set their level of privacy based on the value of k [75, 79]. This means that, given the overhead of the anonymizer, a small value of k could be used to increase the efficiency. Conversely, a large value of k could be chosen to improve the privacy, if the users felt that their position data could be used maliciously. Choosing a value for k, however, seems unnatural. There have been efforts to make the process less artificial by adding the concept of feeling-based privacy [74, 110]. Instead of specifying a k, they propose that the user specifies a cloaking region that they feel will protect their privacy, and the system sets the number of cells for the region based on the popularity of the area. The popularity is computed by using an historical footprint database that the server collected.

New privacy metrics have been proposed that captures the users' privacy with respect to LBSs [22]. The authors begin by analyzing the shortcomings of simple k-anonymity in the context of location queries. Next, they propose privacy metrics that enable the users to specify values that better match their query privacy requirements. From these privacy metrics they also propose spatial generalization algorithms that coincide with the user's privacy requirements.

Methods have also been proposed to confuse and distort the location data, which include path and position confusion. Path confusion was proposed by Hoh and Gruteser [59]. The basic idea is to add uncertainty to the location data of the users at the points the paths of the users cross, making it hard to trace users based on raw location data that was k-anonymized. Position confusion has also been proposed as an approach to provide privacy [64, 79]. The idea is for the trusted anonymizer to group the users according to a cloaking region (CR), thus making it harder for the LS to identify an individual. A common problem with general CR techniques is that there may exist some semantic information about the geography of a location that gives away the user's location. For example, it would not make sense for a user to be on the water without some kind of boat. Also, different people may find certain places sensitive. Damiani et al. have proposed a framework that consists of an obfuscation engine that takes a user's profile, which contains places that the user deems sensitive, and outputs obfuscated locations based on aggregation algorithms [31].

As solutions based on the use of a central anonymizer are not practical, Hashem and Kulik proposed a scheme whereby a group of trusted users construct an ad-hoc network and the task of querying the LS is delegated to a single user [58]. This idea improves on the previous work by the fact that there is no single point of failure. If a user that is querying the LS suddenly goes offline, then another candidate can easily be found. However, generating a trusted ad-hoc network in a real-world scenario is not always possible.

Another method for avoiding the use of a trusted anonymizer is to use "dummy" locations [35, 65]. The basic idea is to confuse the location of the user by sending many random different locations to the server, such that the server cannot distinguish the actual location from the fake locations. This incurs both processing and communication overhead for the user device. The user has to randomly choose a set of fake locations as well as transmit them over a network, wasting bandwidth. We refer the interested reader to Krumm [66], for a more detailed survey in this area.

Most of the previously discussed issues are solved with the introduction of a private information retrieval (PIR) location scheme [49]. The basic idea is to employ PIR to enable the user to query the location database without compromising the privacy of the query. Generally speaking, PIR schemes allow a user to retrieve data (bit or block) from a database, without disclosing the index of the data to be retrieved to the database server [25]. Ghinita et al. used a variant of PIR which is based on the quadratic residuosity problem [68]. Basically the quadratic residuosity problem states that it is computationally hard to determine whether a number is a quadratic residue of some composite modulus n ($x^2 = q \ (mod\ n)$), where the factorization of n is unknown.

This idea was extended to provide database protection [47, 48]. This protocol consists of two stages. In the first stage, the user and server use homomorphic encryption to allow the user to privately determine whether his/her location is contained within a cell, without disclosing his/her coordinates to the server. In the second stage, PIR is used to retrieve the data contained within the appropriate cell.

The homomorphic encryption scheme used to privately compare two integers is the Paillier encryption scheme [90]. The Paillier encryption scheme is known to be additively homomorphic and multiplicatively-by-a-constant homomorphic. This means that we can add or scale numbers even when all numbers are encrypted. Both features are used to determine the sign (most significant bit) of $(a - b)$, and hence the user is able to determine the cell in which he/she is located, without disclosing his/her location.

In this chapter, we describe a protocol for location-based queries given by Paulet, Kaosar, Yi and Bertino [92, 93] that has major performance improvements with respect to the approach by Ghinita et al. [47] and [48]. Like such protocol, the protocol described here is organized according to two stages. In the first stage, the user privately determines his/her location within a public grid, using oblivious transfer. This data contains both the ID and associated symmetric key for the block of data in the private grid. In the second stage, the user executes a communicational efficient PIR [40], to retrieve the appropriate block in the private grid. This block is decrypted using the symmetric key obtained in the previous stage.

The protocol in [92, 93] thus provides protection for both the user and the server. The user is protected because the server is unable to determine his/her location. Similarly, the server's data is protected since a malicious user can only decrypt the block of data obtained by PIR with the encryption key acquired in the previous stage. In other words, users cannot gain any more data than what they have paid for.

The rest of the chapter is organized as follows. Section 4.2 presents the protocol model and other preliminaries. Section 4.3 describes the protocol from [92, 93]. Section 4.4 analyses the security of the protocol. Section 4.5 analyses the performance and efficiency of the protocol. Section 4.6 reports the performance results of a working prototype using two platforms—a desktop and a mobile—and discusses feasibility. Section 4.7 summarizes the chapter and future directions. The presentation in this chapter is partially based on [93].

4.2 MODEL

Before describing the protocol we introduce the system model, which defines the major entities and their roles. The description of the protocol model begins with the notations and system parameters.

4.2.1 NOTATIONS

Let $x \leftarrow y$ be the assignment of the value of variable y to variable x and $E \Leftarrow v$ be the transfer of the variable v to entity E. Denote the ElGamal [36] encryption of message m as $E(m, y) = \boldsymbol{A} = (A_1, A_2) = (g^r, g^m y^r)$, where g is a generator of group G, y is the public key of the form $y = g^x$, and r is chosen at random. This will be used as a basis for constructing an adaptive oblivious transfer scheme [83]. Note that $\boldsymbol{A}$ is a vector, while A_1, A_2 are elements of the vector. The cyclic group G_0 is a multiplicative subgroup of the finite field F_p, where p is a large prime number and q is a prime that divides $(p-1)$. Let g_0 be a generator of group G_0, with order q. Let G_1 be a multiplicative subgroup of finite field F_q, with distinct generators g_1 and g_2 where both have prime order q', where $q' | (q-1)$. Based on this definition, groups G_0 and G_1 can then be linked together and have the form $g_0^{g_1^x g_2^y}$, where x and y are variable integers. This will be used in the application to generate an ElGamal cryptosystem instance in group G_1. We denote $|p|$ to be the bit length of p, $\oplus$ to be the exclusive OR operator, $a||b$ to be the concatenation of a and b, and $\langle |g| \rangle$ to be the order of generator g.

For security reasons, it is required that $|q'| = 1024$ and p has the form $p = 2q' + 1$. It is also required that the parameters $G_0, g_0, G_1, g_1, g_2, p, q'$ are fixed for the duration of a round of the protocol and be made publicly accessible to every entity in the protocol.

4.2.2 SYSTEM MODEL

The system model consists of three types of entities (see Figure 4.1): the set of users[1] who wish to access location data U, a mobile service provider SP, and a location server LS. From the point

[1]In this section we use the term "user" to refer to the entity issuing queries and retrieving query results. In most cases, such user is a client software executing on behalf of a human user.

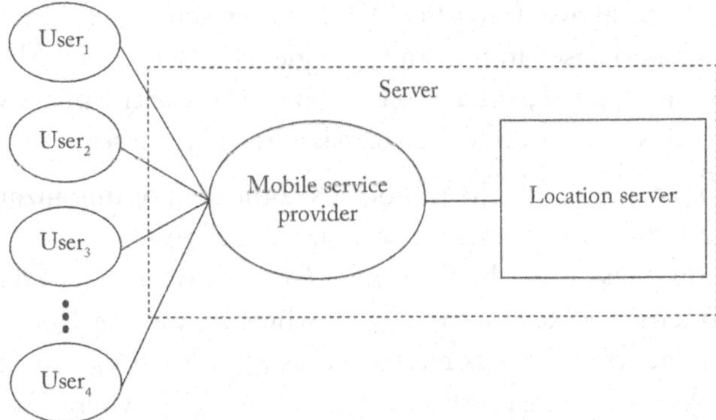

Figure 4.1: System model.

of view of a user, the SP and LS will compose a server, which will serve both functions. The user does not need to be concerned with the specifics of the communication.

The users in the model use some location-based service provided by the location server LS. For example, what is the nearest ATM or restaurant? The purpose of the mobile service provider SP is to establish and maintain the communication between the location server and the user. The location server LS owns a set of POI records r_i for $1 \leqslant i \leqslant \rho$, where ρ is the total number of the records. Each record r_i describes a POI, giving GPS coordinates to its location (x_{gps}, y_{gps}), and a description or name about what is at the location.

It is reasonably assumed that the mobile service provider SP is a passive entity and is not allowed to collude with the LS. We make this assumption because the SP can determine the whereabouts of a mobile device, which, if allowed to collude with the LS, completely subverts any method for privacy. There is simply no technological method for preventing this attack. As a consequence of this assumption, the user is able to either use GPS (Global Positioning System) or the mobile service provider to acquire his/her coordinates.

Since assuming that the mobile service provider SP is trusted to maintain the connection, only two possible adversaries are considered, one for each communication direction. In one case, the user is the adversary and tries to obtain more than he/she is allowed. In another case, the location server LS is the adversary, and tries to uniquely associate a user with a grid coordinate.

4.2.3 SECURITY MODEL

Before giving the definition for the security of the protocol, the concept of k out of N adaptive OT is introduced as follows.

Definition 4.1 (k out of N adaptive oblivious transfer ($OT_{k\times 1}^N$)). $OT_{k\times 1}^N$ protocols contain two phases, for initialization and for transfer. The initialization phase is run by the sender (Bob) who owns the N data elements $X_1, X_2, ..., X_N$. Bob typically computes a commitment to each of the

N data elements, with a total overhead of $O(N)$. He then sends the commitments to the receiver (Alice). The transfer phase is used to transmit a single data element to Alice. At the beginning of each transfer Alice has an input I, and her output at the end of the phase should be data element X_I. An $OT^N_{k\times 1}$ protocol supports up to k successive transfer phases.

Built on the above definition, the protocol is composed of initialization phase and transfer phase. The steps required for the phases are outlined as follows.

The initialization phase is run by the sender (server), who owns a database of location data records and a two dimensional key matrix $\mathcal{K}_{m\times n}$, where m and n are rows and columns, respectively. An element in the key matrix is referenced as $k_{i,j}$. Each $k_{i,j}$ in the key matrix uniquely encrypts one record. A set of prime powers $\mathcal{S} = \{p_1^{c_1}, ..., p_N^{c_N}\}$, where N is the number of blocks, is available to the public. In $\mathcal{S}$, p_i is a prime and c_i is a small natural number such that $p_i^{c_i}$ is longer than the block size in terms of bits (where each block contains a number of POI records). It is required, for convenience, that the elements of $\mathcal{S}$ follow a predictable pattern. In addition, the server sets up a common security parameter k for the system.

The transfer phase is constructed using six algorithms: QG1, RG1, RR1, QG2, RG2, RR2. The first three compose the first phase (Oblivious Transfer Phase), while the last three compose the second phase (Private Information Retrieval Phase). The following six algorithms are executed sequentially and are formally described as follows.

Oblivious Transfer Phase

1. $QueryGeneration_1$ (*Client*) (QG1):
   Takes as input indices i, j, and the dimensions of the key matrix m, n, and outputs a query $\mathcal{Q}_1$ and secret s_1, denoted as $(\mathcal{Q}_1, s_1) = QG_1(i, j, m, n)$.

2. $ResponseGeneration_1$(*Server*) (RG1):
   Takes as input the key matrix $\mathcal{K}_{m\times n}$, and the query $\mathcal{Q}_1$, and outputs a response $\mathcal{R}_1$, denoted as $(\mathcal{R}_1) = RG_1(\mathcal{K}_{m\times n}, \mathcal{Q}_1)$.

3. $ResponseRetrieval_1$ (*Client*) (RR1):
   Takes as input indices i, j, the dimensions of the key matrix m, n, the query $\mathcal{Q}_1$ and the secret s_1, and the response $\mathcal{R}_1$, and outputs a cell-key $k_{i,j}$ and cell-id $ID_{i,j}$, denoted as $(k_{i,j}, ID_{i,j}) = RR_1(i, j, m, n, (\mathcal{Q}_1, s_1), \mathcal{R}_1)$.

Private Information Retrieval Phase

4. $QueryGeneration_2$ (*Client*) (QG2):
   Takes as input the cell-id $ID_{i,j}$, and the set of prime powers $\mathcal{S}$, and outputs a query $\mathcal{Q}_2$ and secret s_2, denoted as $(\mathcal{Q}_2, s_2) = QG_2(ID_{i,j}, \mathcal{S})$.

5. $ResponseGeneration_2$ (*Server*) (RG2):
   Takes as input the database D, the query $\mathcal{Q}_2$, and the set of prime powers $\mathcal{S}$, and outputs a response $\mathcal{R}_2$, denoted as $(\mathcal{R}_2) = RG_2(D, \mathcal{Q}_2, \mathcal{S})$.

6. $ResponseRetrieval_2$ (*Client*) (RR2):
   Takes as input the cell-key $k_{i,j}$ and cell-id $ID_{i,j}$, the query $\mathcal{Q}_2$ and secret s_2, the response $\mathcal{R}_2$, and outputs the data d, denoted as $(d) = RR_2(k_{i,j}, ID_{i,j}, (\mathcal{Q}_2, s_2), \mathcal{R}_2)$.

The transfer phase can be repeatedly used to retrieve points of interest from the location database.

With these functions described, the security definitions for both the client and server can be described as follows.

Definition 4.2 (Client's Security (Indistinguishability)). In a $OT^N_{k\times 1}$ protocol, for any step $1 \leqslant t \leqslant k$, for any previous items $I_1, ..., I_{t-1}$ that the receiver has obtained in the first t-1 transfers, for any $1 \leqslant I_t, I'_t \leqslant N$ and for any probabilistic polynomial time $\mathcal{B}'$ executing the server's part, the views that $\mathcal{B}'$ sees in case the client tries to obtain X_{I_t} and in the case the client tries to obtain $X_{I'_t}$ are computationally indistinguishable given $X_1, X_2, \cdots, X_N$.

Definition 4.3 (Server's Security (Comparison with Ideal Model)). We compare an $OT^N_{k\times 1}$ protocol to the *ideal implementation*, using a trusted third party that gets the server's input $X_1, X_2, ..., X_N$ and the client's requests and gives the client the data elements she has requested. For every probabilistic polynomial-time machine $\mathcal{A}'$ substituting the client, there exists a probabilistic polynomial-time machine $\mathcal{A}''$ that plays the receiver's role in the ideal model such that the outputs of $\mathcal{A}'$ and $\mathcal{A}''$ are computationally indistinguishable.

The above definitions are the same as the definitions for oblivious transfer given in Chapter 1. They are first given in [83].

4.3 PRIVACY-PRESERVING LOCATION-BASED QUERY

We now describe the protocol. We first give a protocol summary to contextualize the proposed solution and then describe the solution's protocol in more detail.

4.3.1 PROTOCOL SUMMARY

The ultimate goal of the protocol is to obtain a set (block) of POI records from the LS, which are close to the user's position, without compromising the privacy of the user or the data stored at the server. This is achieved by applying a two-stage approach shown in Figure 4.2. The first stage is based on a two-dimensional oblivious transfer [83] and the second stage is based on a communicationally efficient PIR [40]. The oblivious transfer based protocol is used by the user to obtain the cell ID, where the user is located, and the corresponding symmetric key. The knowledge of the cell ID and the symmetric key is then used in the PIR-based protocol to obtain and decrypt the location data.

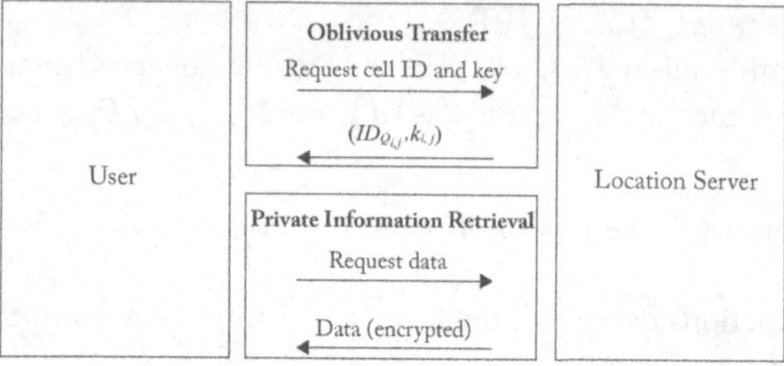

Figure 4.2: High level overview of the protocol.

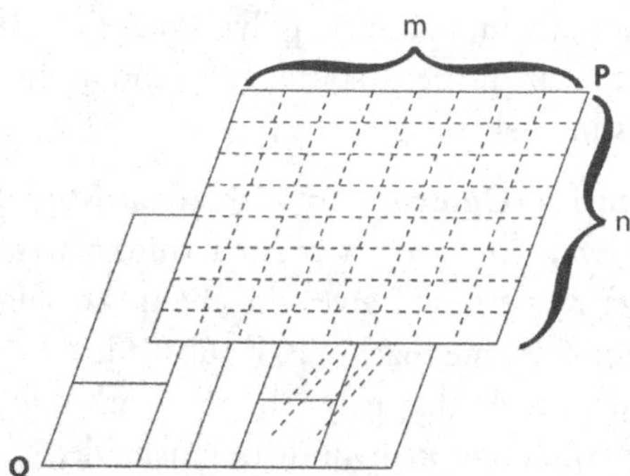

Figure 4.3: The public grid superimposed over the private grid.

The user determines his/her location within a publicly generated grid P by using his/her GPS coordinates and forms an oblivious transfer query.[2] The minimum dimensions of the public grid are defined by the server and are made available to all users of the system. This public grid superimposes over the privately partitioned grid generated by the location server's POI records, such that for each cell $Q_{i,j}$ in the server's partition there is at least one $P_{i,j}$ cell from the public grid. This is illustrated in Figure 4.3.

Since PIR does not require that a user is constrained to obtain only one bit/block, the location server needs to implement some protection for its records. This is achieved by encrypting each record in the POI database with a key using a symmetric key algorithm, where the key for encryption is the same key used for decryption. This key is augmented with the cell info data retrieved by the oblivious transfer query. Hence, even if the user uses PIR to obtain more than one record, the data will be meaningless resulting in improved security for the server's database. Before we describe the protocol in detail, we describe some initialization performed by both parties.

[2]An oblivious transfer query is such that a server cannot learn the user's query, while the user cannot gain more than they are entitled. This is similar to PIR, but oblivious transfer requires protection for the user and server. PIR only requires that the user is protected.

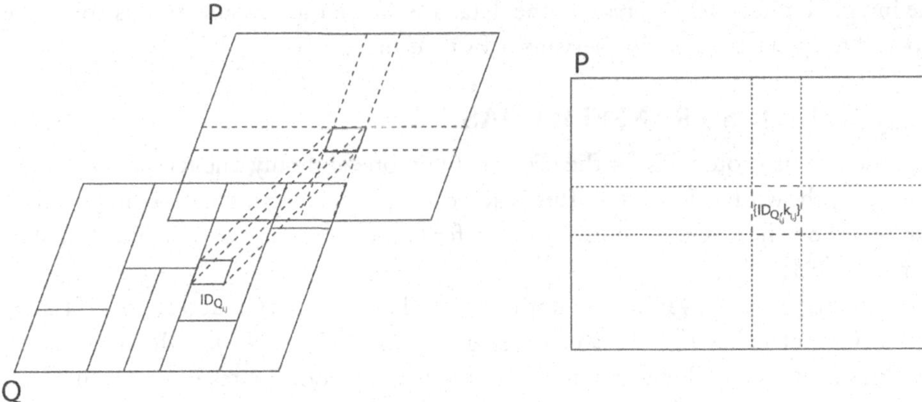

Figure 4.4: Association between the public and private grids.

4.3.2 INITIALIZATION

A user u from the set of users U initiates the protocol process by deciding a suitable square cloaking region CR, which contains his/her location. All user queries will be with respect to this cloaking region. The user also decides on the accuracy of this cloaking region by how many cells are contained within it, where the geographical size of each cell cannot be smaller than the geographical size used in the server's private grid. This information is combined with the dimensions of the CR to form the public grid P and submitted to the location server, which partitions its records or superimposes it over pre-partitioned records (see Figure 4.3). This partition is denoted Q (note that the cells don't necessarily need to be the same size as the cells of P). Each cell in the partition Q must have the same number r_{max} of POI records. Any variation in this number could lead to the server identifying the user. If this constraint cannot be satisfied, then dummy records can be used to make sure each cell has the same amount of data. We assume that the LS does not populate the private grid with misleading or incorrect data, since such action would result in the loss of business under a payment model.

Next, the server encrypts each record r_i within each cell of Q, $Q_{i,j}$, with an associated symmetric key $k_{i,j}$. The encryption keys are stored in a small (virtual) database table that associates each cell in the public grid P, $P_{i,j}$, with both a cell in the private grid $Q_{i,j}$ and corresponding symmetric key $k_{i,j}$. This is shown by Figure 4.4.

The server then processes the encrypted records within each cell $Q_{i,j}$ such that the user can use an efficient PIR [40] to query the records. Using the private partition Q, the server represents each associated (encrypted) data as an integer C_i, with respect to the cloaking region. For each C_i, the server chooses a set of unique prime powers $\pi_i = p_i^{c_i}$, such that $C_i < \pi_i$. We note that the c_i in the exponent must be small for the protocol to work efficiently. Finally, the server uses the Chinese Remainder Theorem to find the smallest integer e such that $e = C_i \ (mod \ \pi_i)$ for all

C_i. The integer e effectively represents the database. Once the initialization is complete, the user can proceed to query the location server for POI records.

4.3.3 OBLIVIOUS TRANSFER PHASE

The purpose of this protocol is for the user to obtain one and only one record from the cell in the public grid P, shown in Figure 4.4. This is achieved by constructing a two dimensional oblivious transfer, based on the ElGamal oblivious transfer [7], using adaptive oblivious transfer proposed by Naor et al. [83].

The public grid P, known by both parties, has m columns and n rows. Each cell in P contains a symmetric key $k_{i,j}$ and a cell id in grid Q or $(ID_{Q_{i,j}}, k_{i,j})$, which can be represented by a stream of bits $X_{i,j}$. The user determines his/her i, j coordinates in the public grid which is used to acquire the data from the cell within the grid. The protocol is initialized by the server by generating $m \times n$ keys of the form $g_0^{g_1^{R_i} g_2^{C_j}}$. This initialization is presented in Algorithm 4.1.

Algorithm 4.1 *Initialization*

Input: $X_{1,1}, ..., X_{m,n}$, where $X_{i,j} = ID_{Q_{i,j}} || k_{i,j}$
Output: $Y_{1,1}, ..., Y_{m,n}$

1: $K_{i,j} \leftarrow K_{i,j} = g_0^{g_1^{R_i} g_2^{C_j}}$, for $1 \leqslant i \leqslant n$ and $1 \leqslant j \leqslant m$, where R_i and C_j are randomly chosen
2: $Y_{i,j} \leftarrow X_{i,j} \oplus H(K_{i,j})$, for $1 \leqslant i \leqslant n$ and $1 \leqslant j \leqslant m$, where H is a fast secure hash function
3: **return** $Y_{1,1}, ..., Y_{m,n}$ {Encryptions of $X_{1,1}, ..., X_{m,n}$ using $K_{i,j}$}

Algorithm 4.1 is executed once and the output $Y_{1,1}, ..., Y_{m,n}$ is sent to the user. At which point, the user can query this information using the indices i, and j, as input. This protocol is presented in Algorithm 4.2.

At the conclusion of the protocol presented by Algorithm 4.2, the user has the information to query the location server for the associated block.

Theorem 4.1 **(Correctness).** *Assume that the user and server follow Algorithms 4.1 and 4.2 correctly. Let $X_{i,j}$ be the bit string encoding the pair $(ID_{Q_{i,j}}, k_{i,j})$ and let $X'_{i,j}$ the bit string generated by Algorithm 4.2 (Step 19) as $X'_{i,j} = Y_{i,j} \oplus H(K_{i,j})$. Then $X'_{i,j} = X_{i,j}$.*

Proof. We begin this proof by showing that $K_{i,j} = K'_{i,j}$, where $K'_{i,j}$ is the key obtained by the user according to the Algorithm 4.2 (step 18). In the initialization algorithm (4.1) $K_{i,j}$ is calculated as $K_{i,j} = g_0^{g_1^{R_i} g_2^{C_j}}$. At the end of the transfer protocol, the user computes $K'_{i,j}$ as $\gamma^{W_3 W_4}$, where W_3 can be simplified as follows when $i = \alpha$.

Algorithm 4.2 *Transfer*

Input: User: i, j

Output: User:$(ID_{Q_{i,j}}, k_{i,j})$

User $(QG1)$
$y_1 \leftarrow g_1^{x_1}$, where y_1 is the public key for the row and x_1 is chosen at random
$y_2 \leftarrow g_2^{x_2}$, where y_2 is the public key for the column and x_2 is chosen at random
$\mathbf{C_1} \leftarrow (A_1, B_1) = (g_1^{r_1}, g_1^{-i} y_1^{r_1})$, where r_1 is chosen at random
$\mathbf{C_2} \leftarrow (A_2, B_2) = (g_2^{r_2}, g_2^{-j} y_2^{r_2})$, where r_2 is chosen at random
$Server \Leftarrow \mathbf{C_1}, \mathbf{C_2}$
Server $(RG1)$
$\mathbf{C'_{1,\alpha}} \leftarrow (A_1^{r'_\alpha}, g_1^{R_\alpha} r_R (g_1^\alpha B_1)^{r'_\alpha})$ for $1 \leqslant \alpha \leqslant n$ and $r_R = g_1^s$, where s, r'_α are chosen at random
$\mathbf{C'_{2,\beta}} \leftarrow (A_2^{r'_\beta}, g_2^{C_\beta} r_C (g_2^\beta B_2)^{r'_\beta})$ for $1 \leqslant \beta \leqslant m$ and $r_C = g_2^t$, where t, r'_β are chosen at random
$\gamma \leftarrow g_0^{1/r_R r_C}$
$User \Leftarrow \mathbf{C'_{1,1}}, ..., \mathbf{C'_{1,n}}, \mathbf{C'_{2,1}}, ..., \mathbf{C'_{2,m}}, \gamma$
User $(RR1)$
Let $(U_{1,i}, V_{1,i}) = \mathbf{C'_{1,i}}$ and $(U_{2,j}, V_{2,j}) = \mathbf{C'_{1,j}}$
$W_1 \leftarrow U_{1,i}^{-x_1}$
$W_2 \leftarrow U_{2,j}^{-x_2}$
$W_3 \leftarrow V_{1,i} W_1$
$W_4 \leftarrow V_{2,j} W_2$
$K'_{i,j} \leftarrow \gamma^{W_3 W_4}$
$X'_{i,j} \leftarrow Y_{i,j} \oplus H(K'_{i,j})$
Reconstruct $(ID_{Q_{i,j}}, k_{i,j})$ from $X'_{i,j}$
return $(ID_{Q_{i,j}}, k_{i,j})$ {Cell id of grid Q, with associated cell key}

$$
\begin{aligned}
W_3 &= V_{1,i} W_1 \\
&= g_1^{R_i} r_R (g_1^\alpha g_1^{-i} y_1^{r_1})^{r'_1} U_{1,i}^{-x_1} \\
&= g_1^{R_i} r_R (y_1^{r_1 r'_1}) U_{1,i}^{-x_1} \\
&= g_1^{R_i} r_R (g_1^{x r_1 r'_1})(g_1^{r_1 r'_1})^{-x_1} \\
&= g_1^{R_i} r_R (g_1^{x r_1 r'_1})(g_1^{-(x r_1 r'_1)}) \\
&= g_1^{R_i} r_R \ (mod\ q)
\end{aligned}
$$

By similar means we can show that $W_4 = g_2^{C_j} r_C$, when $j = \beta$. So we have the following.

$$
\begin{aligned}
\gamma^{W_3 W_4} &= (g_0^{1/r_R r_C})^{g_1^{R_i} r_R g_2^{C_j} r_C} \\
&= g_0^{g_1^{R_i} g_2^{C_j}} \pmod p
\end{aligned}
$$

This proves $K_{i,j} = K'_{i,j}$. Since $\oplus$ is self inverse and given that $Y_{i,j} = X_{i,j} \oplus H(K_{i,j})$, it follows that $X_{i,j} = Y_{i,j} \oplus H(K_{i,j})$. Using knowledge of $K'_{i,j}$, the user can compute $X_{i,j}$, which is the same as $X'_{i,j}$ as desired. This completes the proof. □

4.3.4 PRIVATE INFORMATION RETRIEVAL PHASE

With the knowledge about which cells are contained in the private grid, and the knowledge of the key that encrypts the data in the cell, the user can initiate a private information retrieval protocol with the location server to acquire the encrypted POI data. Assuming the server has initialized the integer e, the user u_i and LS can engage in the following private information retrieval protocol using the $ID_{Q_{i,j}}$, obtained from the execution of the previous protocol, as input. The $ID_{Q_{i,j}}$ allows the user to choose the associated prime number power π_i, which in turn allows the user to query the server. The protocol is presented in Algorithm 4.3.

Algorithm 4.3 *PIRProtocol*

Input: **User:**$ID_{Q_{i,j}}$
Output: **User:**C_i

User (*QG2*)
$\pi_0 \leftarrow \pi_i$, where π_i is chosen based on the value of $ID_{Q_{i,j}}$
Generate random group G and group element g, such that π_0 divides the order of g
$q \leftarrow |\langle g \rangle| / \pi_0$
$h \leftarrow g^q$
$Server \Leftarrow G, g$
Server (*RG2*)
$g_e \leftarrow g^e$
$User \Leftarrow g_e$
User (*RR2*)
$h_e \leftarrow g_e^q$
$C_i \leftarrow log_h h_e$, where $\log_h$ is the discrete log base h
return C_i {The requested (encrypted) data}

Theorem 4.2 **(Correctness).** *Assume that the user and the server follow the protocol correctly, then the user successfully acquires C_i for his/her chosen prime index.*

Proof. It is easy to see that $C_i = e \ (mod \ \pi_i)$ and $h_e = g_e^{|\langle g \rangle|/\pi_i}$. Then C_i is the discrete logarithm of h_e to the base h, since $g_e^{|\langle g \rangle|/\pi_i} = g^{e|\langle g \rangle|/\pi_i} = g^{e_{\pi_i}|\langle g \rangle|/\pi_i} = h^{e_{\pi_i}}$, where e_{π_i} stands for $e \ (mod \ \pi_i)$. This completes the proof. □

At the conclusion of the protocol, the user has successfully acquired the block that contain the encrypted POI records. With the knowledge of the cell key $k_{i,j}$, the user can decrypt C_i and obtain the requested data, thus concluding one round of the protocol. Using the same set-up, the user can execute several more rounds very efficiently and effectively without compromising his/her privacy. Similarly, the server's data remains protected based on the fact the user can only acquire one key per round. The security is analysed in more detail next.

4.4 SECURITY ANALYSIS

In this section, we analyse the security of the client and the server. While the client does not want to give up the privacy of his/her location, the server does not want to disclose other records to the client. This would not make much business sense in a variety of applications. The analysis will be with respect to the security definitions in Section 4.2.3.

4.4.1 CLIENT'S SECURITY

Fundamentally, the information that is most valuable to the user is his/her location. This location is mapped to a cell $P_{i,j}$. In both phases of the protocol, the oblivious transfer-based protocol and the private information retrieval-based protocol, the server must not be able to distinguish two queries of the client from each other. We will now describe both cases separately.

In the oblivious transfer phase, each coordinate of the location is encrypted by the ElGamal encryption scheme, e.g., $(g_1^{r_1}, g_1^{-i} y_1^{r_1})$. It has been shown that ElGamal encryption scheme is semantically secure [36]. This means that given the encryption of one of two plaintexts m_1 and m_2 chosen by a challenger, the challenger cannot determine which plaintext is encrypted, with probability significantly greater than 1/2 (the success rate of random guessing). In view of it, the server cannot distinguish any two queries of the client from each other in this phase.

In the private information retrieval phase, the security of the client is built on the Gentry-Ramzan private information retrieval protocol, which is based on the phi-hiding (ϕ-hiding) assumption [40].

On the basis of the above security analysis, we can conclude with the following theorem.

Theorem 4.3 *Assume that the ElGamal encryption scheme is semantically secure and the Gentry-Ramzan PIR has client security, the protocol given by Paulet, Kaosar, Yi and Bertino has client's security, i.e., the server cannot distinguish any two queries of the client from each other.*

4.4.2 SERVER'S SECURITY

Intuitively, the server's security requires that the client can retrieve one record only in each query to the server, and the server must not disclose other records to the client in the response. Our protocol achieves the server's security in the oblivious transfer phase, which is built on the Naor-Pinkas oblivious transfer protocol [83].

Algorithms 4.1 and 4.2 follow the same methodology as the Naor-Pinkas adaptive oblivious transfer protocol, except that the transfer phase is constructed using the ElGamal encryption scheme. In the generation of the first response (RG_1), the server computes $C'_{1,\alpha} = (A_1^{r'_\alpha}, g_1^{R_\alpha} r_R (g_1^\alpha B_1)^{r'_\alpha})$ for $1 \leqslant \alpha \leqslant n$, where $B_1 = g_1^{-i} y_1^{r_1}$, and sends $C'_{1,\alpha}$ $(1 \leqslant \alpha \leqslant n)$ to the client. Only when $\alpha = i$, $C'_{1,i} = (g_1^{r_i r'_i}, g_1^{R_i} r_R y_1^{r_i r'_i})$ is the encryption of $g_1^{R_i} r_R$. When $\alpha \neq i$, $C'_{1,\alpha}$ is the encryption of $g_1^{R_\alpha} r_R g_1^{r'_\alpha}$, where r'_α is unknown to the client. Because the discrete logarithm is hard, the client cannot determine r'_α from $A_1^{r'_\alpha}$. Therefore, $g_1^{R_\alpha} r_R$ is blinded by the random factor $g_1^{r'_\alpha}$. In view of it, the client can retrieve the useful $g_1^{R_i} r_R$ only from $C'_{1,\alpha}$ $(1 \leqslant \alpha \leqslant n)$. Then following the Naor-Pinkas oblivious transfer protocol, the client can retrieve the encryption key $k_{i,j}$ only in the end of the phase.

In the private information retrieval phase, even if the client can retrieve more than one encrypted records, he/she can decrypt only one record with the encryption key $k_{i,j}$ retrieved in the first phase.

Based on the above analysis, we obtain the following result.

Theorem 4.4 *Assume that the discrete logarithm is hard and the Naor-Pinkas protocol is a secure oblivious transfer protocol, the protocol given by Paulet, Kaosar, Yi and Bertino has server's security.*

4.5 PERFORMANCE ANALYSIS

An extensive performance analysis has been carried out to show that the protocol given by Paulet, Kaosar, Yi and Bertino (for brevity, PKYB) is very practical [93]. The performance analysis consists of the computation analysis and the communication analysis. The protocol has also been compared with the protocol by Ghinita et al. [48] (for brevity, GKKB).

4.5.1 COMPUTATION

Since the most expensive operation in the PKYB protocol is the modular exponentiation, the protocol implementation has been optimized by minimizing the number of times it is required. The implementation assumes that some components can be precomputed, and hence one only needs to consider the computations needed at runtime. Furthermore, the number of exponentiations required by the PIR protocol is reduced to the number of multiplications that are required. This will make the computational comparison between the PKYB and GKKB protocols easier to describe.

The transfer protocol is initiated by the user, who chooses indices i and j. According to the PKYB protocol the user needs to compute $(A_1, B_1) = (g_1^{r_1}, g_1^{-i} y_1^{r_1})$ and $(A_2, B_2) = (g_2^{r_2}, g_2^{-j} y_2^{r_2})$. Since the user knows the discrete logarithm of both y_1 and y_2 (i.e., x_1 and x_2 respectively), the user can compute (A_1, B_1) and (A_2, B_2) as $(A_1, B_1) = (g_1^{r_1}, g_1^{-i+x_1r_1})$ and $(A_2, B_2) = (g_2^{r_2}, g_2^{-j+x_2r_2})$ respectively. Hence, the user has to compute four exponentiations to generate his/her query.

Upon receiving the user's query, the server needs to compute $((A_1)^{r'_\alpha}, g_1^{R_\alpha} r_R (g_1^\alpha (A_2))^{r'_\alpha})$ for $1 \leqslant \alpha \leqslant n$ and $((B_1)^{r'_\beta}, g_2^{C_\beta} r_C (g_2^\beta (B_2))^{r'_\beta})$ for $1 \leqslant \beta \leqslant m$. Since g^α and g^β can be pre-computed and the server knows the discrete log of r_R and r_C, the server has to compute $3n + 3m$ exponentiations, plus an additional exponentiation for computing γ.

The user requires three additional exponentiations to determine $K_{i,j}$. After the user has determined $K_{i,j}$, he/she can determine $X_{i,j}$ and proceed with the PIR protocol. This protocol requires three more exponentiations, two performed by the user and one performed by the server. In terms of multiplications, the user has to perform $2|N|$ operations and the server has to perform $|e|$ operations. The user also has to compute the discrete logarithm base h, $\log_h$, of h_e. This process can be expedited by using the Pohlig-Hellman discrete logarithm algorithm [94]. The running time of the Pohlig-Hellman algorithm is proportional to the factorization of the group order $O(\sum_{i=1}^{r} c_i(\log n + \sqrt{p_i}))$, where r is the number of unique factors and n is the order of the group. In the PKYB protocol, the order of the group is $\pi_i = p_i^{c_i}$ and the number of unique factors is $r = 1$, resulting in running time $O(c(\log p^c + \sqrt{p}))$.

The comparison shows that the PKYB protocol is computationally more efficient than the GKKB protocol. The latter uses the homomorphic properties of the Paillier encryption scheme [90] in order to test whether a user is located in a cell or not. This requires the user to perform four exponentiations to compute the ciphertext of his/her coordinates, x and y. The server then has to compute $(4 \times (n \times m))$. The user has to decrypt at most all these ciphertexts $(4 \times (n \times m))$.

Once the user has determined his/her cell index he/she can proceed with the PIR protocol (described in [49]) to retrieve the data. The PIR is based on the Quadratic Residuosity Problem [68], which allows the user to privately query the database. Let t be the total number of bits in the database, where there are a rows and b columns. The user and server have to compute $2(\sqrt{a \times b}) \times \frac{|N|}{2}$ and $a \times b$ multiplications respectively. We remark that multiplying the whole database by a string of numbers, which is required by the PIR protocol based on the quadratic residuosity problem, is equivalent to computing g^e in the PKYB protocol. The size of number e is principally defined by the prime powers. In general, it takes about $\eta = \sum_{i=1}^{N} log_2(\pi_i)$ bits to store e and we would expect to be multiplying $\eta/2$ of the time using the square-and-multiply method for fast exponentiation. This is roughly equivalent to $a \times b$ multiplications as required in the GKKB protocol.

4.5.2 COMMUNICATION

Since the PKYB protocol requires the discrete logarithm to be intractable for security reasons, in the experiments, q' is set to be 1024 bits, which makes p roughly 1025 bits. Since q' and p are about the same size we set a common L as 1024 bits for analysis. In the PKYB protocol, the user needs $4L$ communications, while the server requires $2(m+n)2L + L$ communications in the oblivious transfer protocol. In the PIR protocol, the user and server exchange one group element each.

Since the GKKB protocol uses the Paillier encryption scheme, the size of one ciphertext in their scheme is $2L$. Based on this parameter, the user has to submit $4L$ bits to the server as his/her encrypted location. Then the server has to send $4 \times n \times m \times 2L$, for the user to determine his/her location. For the PIR based on the QRA, the user and server have to send $\sqrt{a \times b} \times L$. The performance analysis for stage 1 (user location test) and stage 2 (PIR) are summarized in Tables 4.1 and 4.2, respectively, where the computation in Table 4.1 is in terms of exponentiation and the computation in Table 4.2 is in terms of multiplication.

Table 4.1: Stage 1 performance analysis summary

		PKYB [93]	GKKB [48]
Computation	User	7	$4 + 4(n \times m)$
	Server	$3n + 3m + 1$	$4(n \times m)$
	Total	$8 + 3n + 3m$	$4 + 4(n \times m) + 4(n \times m)$
Communication		$2(m+n)2L + L$	$4L + 4(m \times n)2L$

Table 4.2: Stage 2 performance analysis summary

		PKYB [93]	GKKB [48]
Computation	User	$O\left(c\left(\lg p^c + \sqrt{p}\right)\right) + 2\|N\|$	$2\left(\sqrt{a \times b}\right) \times \frac{\|N\|}{2}$
	Server	$\|e\|$	$a \times b$
	Total	$O\left(c\left(\lg p^c + \sqrt{p}\right)\right) + 2\|N\| + \|e\|$	$2\left(\sqrt{a + b}\right) \times \frac{\|N\|}{2} + a \times b$
Communication		$2L$	$\sqrt{a \times b} L$

When we analyse the difference in performance between the PKYB and GKKB protocols, we find that the former is more efficient. The performance of the first stage of each protocol is about the same, except that the PKYB protocol requires $O(m + n)$ operations while the GKKB protocol requires $O(m \times n)$. In the second stage, the PKYB protocol is far more efficient with respect to communication, in that it requires the transmission of only two group elements whereas the GKKB protocol requires the exchange of an $a \times b$ matrix.

4.6 EXPERIMENTAL EVALUATION

The PKYB protocol has been implemented on a platform consisting of a desktop machine, running the server software, and a mobile phone, running the client software. For both platforms, the required time for the OT and PIR protocols are measured separately to test the performance of each protocol and the relative performance between the two protocols. The desktop machine that was used in the experiment is equipped with a Intel Core 2 Duo E8200 2.66GHz processor and 2GB of RAM. The implementation on this platform was written using Visual C++ under the Windows XP operating system. The Number Theory Library (NTL) [98] is used for computations requiring large integers and OpenSSL [86] to compute the SHA-1 hash.

The implementation on the mobile phone platform was programmed using the Android Development Platform, which is a Java-based programming environment. The mobile device used was a Sony Xperia S with a Dual-core 1.5 GHz CPU and 1 GB of RAM. The whole solution was executed for 100 trials, where the time taken (in seconds) for each major component was recorded and the average time was calculated. The parameters for the experiment were the same on both platforms, which are described next.

4.6.1 EXPERIMENTAL PARAMETERS

Oblivious Transfer Protocol

In the implementation experiment for the OT protocol, a modified ElGamal instance was generated with a prime p as the modulo such that $|p| = 1024$ and a prime q as the order of the subgroup G of $\mathbb{Z}_p$ such that $|q| \geqslant 320$, $q|(p-1)$, and $q-1$ has a prime factor q' such that $|q'| \geqslant 160$. We randomly choose three integers a, b, c such that $a^{(p-1)/q}(mod\ p) > 1$, $b^{(q-1)/q'}(mod\ q) > 1$, $c^{(q-1)/q'}(mod\ q) > 1$, and set $g_0 = a^{(p-1)/q}(mod\ p)$, $g_1 = b^{(q-1)/q'}(mod\ q)$ and $g_2 = c^{(q-1)/q'}(mod\ q)$. Then g_0 is a generator of the group G and g_1, g_2 are two generators of a subgroup G' of $\mathbb{Z}_q$. The order of the group G' is the prime q'.

The public matrix P was set to be a 25×25 matrix of key and cell index information. The time required to generate a matrix of keys according to Algorithm 4.1 was first measured. This procedure only needs to be executed once for the lifetime of the data. There is a requirement that each hash value of $g_0^{g_1^{R_i} g_2^{C_j}}$ is unique. The SHA-1 is used to compute the hash $H(\cdot)$, and there is negligible probability that a number will repeat in the matrix.

PIR Protocol

In the PIR protocol a 15×15 private matrix is fixed, which contains the data owned by the server. The prime set contains the first 225 primes, starting at 3. The powers for the primes were chosen to allow for at least a block size of 1024 bits ($3^{647}, 5^{442}, \ldots, 1429^{98}$). Random values were chosen for each prime power $e = C_i\ (mod\ \pi_i)$, and the Chinese Remainder Theorem was used to determine the smallest possible e satisfying this system of congruences.

Once the database has been initialized, the user can initiate the protocol by issuing the server his/her query. The query consists of finding a suitable group whose order is divisible by one of the prime powers π_i. This is achieved in a similar manner to Gentry and Ramzan [40]. Primes q_0 and q_1 are chosen to compute "semi-safe" primes $Q_0 = 2q_0\pi_i + 1$ and $Q_1 = 2q_1 + 1$. The modulus is set as $N = Q_0Q_1$ and group order as $\phi(N) = \phi(Q_0Q_1) = (Q_0 - 1)(Q_1 - 1)$. Hence, the order $\phi(N)$ has π_i as a factor. g is set to be a quasi-generator, such that the order of g also has π_i as a factor. In the experiment, $|q_0| = |q_1| = 128$ is set. This results in a modulus N which is roughly 1024 bits in length, which is equivalent to an RSA modulus.

4.6.2 EXPERIMENTAL RESULTS

In both phases of the PKYB protocol, there are three major steps: the user's query, the server's response, and the user decoding. Table 4.3 displays the average runtime on the desktop and mobile platforms, for each component of the oblivious transfer phase. Similarly, Table 4.4 presents the average times for each component of the private information retrieval protocol.

Table 4.3: Oblivious transfer experimental results for desktop and mobile platforms

Component	Desktop	Mobile
$Initialisation_{OT}$	1.70958s	—
$QueryGeneration_1$	—	0.00108s
$ResponseGeneration_1$	0.00969s	—
$ResponseRetrieval_1$	—	0.00004s

Table 4.4: Private information retrieval experimental results for desktop and mobile platforms

Component	Desktop	Mobile
$QueryGeneration_2$	—	23.90666s
$ResponseGeneration_2$	4.57127s	—
$ResponseRetrieval_2$	—	0.49123s

Please note that Tables 4.3 and 4.4 list average time only.

4.7 CONCLUSION

In this chapter we have described a location-based query solution, given by Paulet, Kaosar, Yi and Bertino, that employs two protocols that enables a user to privately determine and acquire location data. The first step is for a user to privately determine his/her location using oblivious transfer on a public grid. The second step involves a private information retrieval interaction that retrieves the record with high communication efficiency.

The performance of their protocol has been analyzed and found to be both computationally and communicationally more efficient than the solution by Ghinita et al., which is the most recent solution.

Future work is expected to test the protocol on many different mobile devices. The mobile result reported by Paulet, Kaosar, Yi and Bertino [93] may be different when deploying the protocol on other mobile devices and software environments. Also, the overhead of the primality test used in the PIR-based protocol needs to be reduced. Additionally, the problem concerning the LS supplying misleading data to the client is also interesting. Privacy preserving reputation techniques seem like a suitable approach to address such problem. A possible solution could integrate methods from [50]. Once suitable strong solutions exist for the general case, they can be easily integrated into the approach by Paulet, Kaosar, Yi and Bertino.

CHAPTER 5

Discussion and Future Work

Private information retrieval (PIR) protocols are designed to safeguard the privacy of database users. They allow clients to retrieve records from public databases while completely hiding the identity of the retrieved records from database owners.

Since the first PIR approach was introduced by Chor, Goldreich, Kushilevitz and Sudan [24] in 1995 in a multi-server setting and the first single-database PIR was introduced by Kushilevitz and Ostrovsky [68] in 1997, many efficient PIR protocols have been discovered. Meanwhile, PIR have been extensively used to the privacy of users in various application.

In this book, we have surveyed classic PIR and OT protocols and presented some constructions of PIR and PBR protocols with fully homomorphic encryption (FHE) given by Yi, Kaosar, Paulet and Bertino [106]. The FHE-based PIR protocols can be made more computationally efficient than other PIR protocols although their communication complexity may be higher than other PIR protocols. Overall, the FHE-based PIR protocol are usually more efficient than other PIR protocols.

In addition, we have presented a solution for private data warehouse query, given by Yi, Paulet and Bertion [107], including a Private Cell Retrieval protocol. The solution allows a user not only to retrieve a cell from data warehouse without revealing to the server which cell is retrieved, but also to perform OLAP operations on the data warehouse without revealing to the server what operations are performed. This can be considered a kind of extension to PIR.

Furthermore, we have presented a solution for private location-based query, given by Paulet, Kaosar, Yi and Bertino [92, 93]. The solution employs two protocols that enable a user to privately determine and acquire location data. The first step is for a user to privately determine his/her location using oblivious transfer on a public grid. The second step involves a private information retrieval interaction that retrieves the record with high communication efficiency.

Recently, we have seen a significant evolution from single-database PIR to private searching on streaming data. The problem of private searching on streaming data was first put forward by Ostrovsky and Skeith [88]. It was motivated by one of the tasks of the intelligence community, to collect potentially useful information from huge volumes of streaming data flowing through a public server. What is potentially useful and raises a red flag is often classified and satisfies secret criteria. The challenge is how to keep the criteria classified even if the program residing in the public server falls into the enemy's hands. This work has many applications for the purposes of intelligence gathering. For example, in airports one can use this technique to find if any of hundreds of passenger lists has a name from the possible terrorists list and if so his/her itinerary without revealing the secret terrorists list.

Private searching on steaming data and single-database PIR have the same aim, that is, retrieving information from a source of data without revealing user's query to the owner of the data. Both of them intend to protect the privacy of the user. The first difference between them is that the data in PIR is fixed while the data in private searching is streaming data. The second difference is that the user in PIR knows the index of the data he wishes to retrieve while the user in private searching only know the searching criteria. The third difference is that the outcome in PIR is immediately returned to the user while the searching results in private searching are stored in a buffer which is returned to the user after certain period.

Compared with PIR, private searching on streaming data is more complicated and difficult to design and implement. The first solution for private searching on streaming data was given by Ostrovsky and Skeith in 2005 [88, 89]. It was built on the concept of public-key program obfuscation, where an obfuscator compiles a given program f from a complexity class $\mathcal{C}$ into a pair of algorithms (F, Dec), such that $Dec(F(x)) = f(x)$ for any input x and it is impossible to distinguish for any polynomial time adversary which f from $\mathcal{C}$ was used to produce a given code for F.

Private searching on streaming data allows us to search for streaming documents containing one or more of classified keywords $K = \{k_1, k_2, \cdots, k_{|K|}\} \subset D$, where D is the dictionary and store the findings in a buffet and send it the user after certain period. Ostrovsky and Skeith [88, 89] suggested to throw the findings into randomly chosen boxes in the buffet. If two different matching documents are ever added to the same buffer box, a collision will occur and both copies will be lost. To avoid the loss of matching documents, the buffer size has to be sufficiently large so that each matching document can survive in at least one buffer box with overwhelming probability.

Bethencourt, Song and Waters proposed a different approach for retrieving matching documents from the buffer [10, 11]. Like the idea of Ostrovsky and Skeith, an encrypted dictionary is used, and non-matching documents have no effect on the contents of the buffer. However, rather than using one large buffer and attempting to avoid collisions, Bethencourt, Song and Water stored the matching documents in three buffers—the data buffer $\mathbb{F}$, the count buffer $\mathbb{C}$, and the matching indices buffer $\mathbb{I}$, and retrieved them by solving linear systems.

The advantage of Bethencourt-Song-Water approach, compared to the Ostrovsky-Skeith solution, is that buffer collisions do not matter because matching documents can be retrieved by solving linear systems. Consequently, the buffer size does not need to be sufficiently large in order to maintain a high probability of recovering all matching documents. In fact, the buffer size becomes optimal, i.e., $O(m)$. However, the Bethencourt-Song-Water approach has a drawback as well. To determine the ordinal numbers of potentially matching documents in the decrypted buffer $\mathbb{I}'$, Bethencourt, Song and Water had to check each of the indices $i \in \{1, 2, \cdots, t\}$ of the data stream. Therefore, the buffer recovering has a running-time proportional to the size of the data stream, i.e., $O(m^{2.376} + t\log(t/m))$. This does not fit the model given in [88, 89], in which the buffer is decrypted at the cost which is independent of the stream size.

In most of the solutions for private searching on streaming data, the searching criteria can be constructed by only simple combinations of keywords, e.g., disjunction of keywords. In some applications, one may wish to search for streaming documents satisfying more complicated searching criteria, for example, finding documents containing conjunctive keywords, or finding documents containing more than k out of n keywords. In 2011, Yi and Bertino proposed some solutions for privately searching conjunctive keywords from streaming data [108] and in 2012, Yi and Xing [109] proposed a threshold solution for privately searching documents which contain more than t out of n keywords.

Future work is expected to explore practical solutions for private searching on streaming data which allows us to search documents satisfying more complicated searching criteria.

Bibliography

[1] C. Aguilar-Melchor and P. Gaborit. A lattice-based computationally-efficient private information retrieval protocol. In *Proc. WEWORC '07*, 2007. DOI: 10.1007/978-3-642-18178-8_10. 19

[2] C. Aguilar-Melchor and P. Gaborit. A fast private information retrieval protocol. In *Proc. ISIT '08*, 2008. DOI: 10.1109/ISIT.2008.4595308. 19, 34

[3] C. Aguilar-Melchor, P. Gaborit and J. Herranz. Additively homomorphic encryption with d-operand multiplications. http://eprint.iacr.org/2008/378. DOI: 10.1007/978-3-642-14623-7_8. 19, 34, 35

[4] A. Ambainis. Upper bound on the communication complexity of private information retrieval. In *Proc. 24th International Colloquium on Automata, Languages and Programming*, pp. 401–407, 1997. DOI: 10.1007/3-540-63165-8_196.

[5] D. Asonov. Private information retrieval - an overview and current trends. In *Proc. ECD-PvA Workshop, Informatik '01*, 2001.

[6] A. Beimel and Y. Ishai. Information-theoretic private information retrieval: a unified construction. In *Proc. 28th International Colloquium on Automata, Languages and Programming*, pages 912–926, 2001. DOI: 10.1007/3-540-48224-5_74. 2

[7] M. Bellare and S. Micali, Non-interactive oblivious transfer and applications. In *Proc. CRYPTO '89*, pages 547–557, 1989. DOI: 10.1007/0-387-34805-0_48. 72

[8] J. Benaloh. Dense probabilistic encryption. In *Proc. the Workshop on Selected Areas of Cryptography*, pages 120–128, 1994. 7

[9] A. Beresford and F. Stajano. Location privacy in pervasive computing. *IEEE Pervasive Computing*, vol. 2, no. 1, pp. 46–55, 2003. DOI: 10.1109/MPRV.2003.1186725. 63

[10] J. Bethencourt, D. Song and B. Water B. New construction and practical applications for private streaming searching. In *Proc. IEEE Symposium on Security and Privacy (SP '06)*, 2006. 84

[11] J. Bethencourt, D. Song and B. Water. New techniques for private stream searching. *ACM Transactions on Information and System Security*, 12(3), 16:1-32, 2009. DOI: 10.1145/1455526.1455529. 84

[12] C. Bettini, X. Wang, and S. Jajodia. Protecting privacy against location-based personal identification. *Secure Data Management*, Lecture Notes in Computer Science, W. Jonker and M. Petkovic, Eds., 2005, vol. 3674, pp. 185–199. DOI: 10.1007/11552338_13. 64

[13] D. Boneh, E. Goh and K. Nissim. Evaluating 2-DNF formulas on ciphertexts. In *Proc. TCC '05*, pp. 325–341, 2005. DOI: 10.1007/978-3-540-30576-7_18. 40, 45, 49, 50, 54, 60

[14] Z. Brakerski, C. Gentry and V. Vaikuntanathan. Fully homomorphic encryption without bootstrapping. http://eprint.iacr.org/2011/277. 20, 35

[15] Z. Brakerski and V. Vaikuntanathan. Efficient fully homomorphic encryption from (standard) LWE. http://eprint.iacr.org/2011/344. DOI: 10.1109/FOCS.2011.12. 20, 35

[16] G. Brassard, C. Crepeau and J.M. Robert. All-or-nothing disclosure of secrets. In *Proc. CRYPTO '86*, pages 234–238, 1986. DOI: 10.1007/3-540-47721-7_17. 3, 10

[17] G. Brassard, C. Crepeau, and M. Santha. Oblivious transfers and intersecting codes. *IEEE Transactions on Information Theory*, pp. 1769–1780, 1996. DOI: 10.1109/18.556673.

[18] C. Cachin, S. Micali, and M. Stadler. Computationally private information retrieval with polylogarithmic communication. In *Proc. EUROCRYPT '99*, pages 402–414, 1999. DOI: 10.1007/3-540-48910-X_28. 1, 2, 3, 8, 17, 20, 34, 40, 53

[19] Jan Camenisch, Maria Dubovitskaya, and Gregory Neven. Oblivious transfer with access controls. In *Proc. ACM CCS '09*, pages 131–140, 2009. DOI: 10.1145/1653662.1653679. 17

[20] Jan Camenisch, Gregory Neven, and abhi shelat. Simulatable adaptive oblivious transfer. In *Proc. EUROCRYPT '07*, pages 573–590, 2007. DOI: 10.1007/978-3-540-72540-4_33. 17

[21] Y. Chang. Single database private information retrieval with logarithmic communication. In *Proc. 9th Australasian Conference on Information Security and Privacy*, pages 50–61, 2004. DOI: 10.1007/978-3-540-27800-9_5. 2, 6, 7, 20, 33

[22] X. Chen and J. Pang, "Measuring query privacy in location-based services", Proc. *CODASPY '12*, pages 49–60, 2012. DOI: 10.1145/2133601.2133608. 64

[23] B. Chor and N. Gilboa. Computational private information retrieval. In *Proc. 29th ACM Symposium on the Theory of Computing*, pages 304–313,1997. DOI: 10.1145/258533.258609.

[24] B. Chor, O. Goldreich, E. Kushilevitz, and M. Sudan. Private information retrieval. In *Proc. 36th IEEE Symposium on Foundations of Computer Science*, pages 41–51, 1995. DOI: 10.1145/293347.293350. 1, 2, 40, 53, 83

[25] B. Chor, E. Kushilevitz, O. Goldreich, and M. Sudan. Private information retrieval. *J. ACM*, vol. 45, no. 6, pp. 965–981, 1998. DOI: 10.1145/293347.293350. 2, 65

[26] C.-K. Chu and W.-G. Tzeng. Efficient k-out-of-n oblivious transfer schemes with adaptive and non-adaptive queries. In *Proc. PKC '05*, pages 172–183, 2005. DOI: 10.1007/978-3-540-30580-4_12.

[27] C.-K. Chu and W.-G. Tzeng. Efficient k-out-of-n oblivious transfer schemes. *Journal of Universal Computer Science*, pages 397–415, 2008. DOI: 10.1007/978-3-540-30580-4_12.

[28] C. Crepeau. Equivalence between two flavors of oblivious transfers. In *Proc. of CRYPTO '87*, pages 350–354, 1988. DOI: 10.1007/3-540-48184-2_30. 10, 16

[29] G. Di Crescenzo, T. Malkin, and R. Ostrovsky. Single-database private information retrieval implies oblivious transfer. In *Proc. EUROCRYPT '00*, pages 122–138, 2000. DOI: 10.1007/3-540-45539-6_10. 3

[30] I. Damgard and M. Jurik. A Generalisation. A simplification and some applications of Paillier's probabilistic public-key system. In *Proc. PKC '01*, pages 119–136, 2001. DOI: 10.1007/3-540-44586-2_9. 2, 20, 49

[31] M. Damiani, E. Bertino, and C. Silvestri. The PROBE Framework for the Personalized Cloaking of Private Locations. *Trans. Data Privacy*, vol. 3, no. 2, pp. 123–148, 2010. 64

[32] C. Devet, I. Goldberg, N. Heninger. Optimally robust private information retrieval. In *Proc. USENIX '12*, pages 13–13, 2012. 2

[33] G. Di Crescenzo, T. Malkin, and R. Ostrovsky. Single database private information retrieval implies oblivious transfer. In *Proc EUROCRYPT '00*, pp. 122–138, 2000. DOI: 10.1007/3-540-45539-6_10. 16

[34] M. Dijk, C. Gentry, S. Halevi and V. Vaikuntanathan. Fully homomorphic encryption over the integers. In *Proc. EUROCRYPT '10*, pages 24–43, 2010. DOI: 10.1007/978-3-642-13190-5_2. 20, 22, 31, 32, 49

[35] M. Duckham and L. Kulik, "A formal model of obfuscation and negotiation for location privacy," Proc. *Pervasive Computing*, Lecture Notes in Computer Science, H. Gellersen, R. Want, and A. Schmidt, Eds., 2005, vol. 3468, pp. 243–251. DOI: 10.1007/11428572_10. 65

[36] T. ElGamal. A public-key cryptosystem and a signature scheme based on discrete logarithms. *IEEE Transactions on Information Theory*, 31 (4): 469–472, 1985. DOI: 10.1109/TIT.1985.1057074. 14, 49, 60, 66, 75

[37] S. Even, O. Goldreich and A. Lempel. A randomized protocol for signing contracts. *Communications of the ACM*, 28(6): 637–647, 1985. DOI: 10.1145/3812.3818. 3, 10, 11, 12

[38] W. Gasarch. A survey on private information retrieval. 2004. 2

[39] Y. Gentner, Y. Ishai, E. Kushilevitz and T. Malkin. Protecting data privacy in private information retrieval schemes. In *Proc. 30th ACM Symposium on Theory of Computing*, pages 151–160, 1998. DOI: 10.1145/276698.276723. 10

[40] C. Gentry and Z. Ramzan. Single database private information retrieval with constant communication rate. In *Proc. ICALP '05*, pages 803–815, 2005. DOI: 10.1007/11523468_65. 2, 3, 8, 20, 33, 34, 40, 53, 65, 69, 71, 75, 80

[41] C. Gentry. *Fully Homomorphic Encryption Scheme*. PhD thesis, Stanford University, 2009. Manuscript available at http://crypto.stanford.edu/craig. 20, 31

[42] C. Gentry. Fully homomorphic encryption using ideal lattices. In *Proc. STOC '09*, pages 169–178, 2009. DOI: 10.1145/1536414.1536440. 20, 49

[43] C. Gentry. Computing arbitrary functions of encrypted data. *Communications of the ACM*, 53(3): 97–105, 2010. DOI: 10.1145/1666420.1666444. 20

[44] C. Gentry. Toward basing fully homomorphic encryption on worst-case hardness. In *Proc. CRYPTO '10*, pages 116–137, 2010. DOI: 10.1007/978-3-642-14623-7_7. 20

[45] C. Gentry and S. Halevi. Implementing Gentry's fully-homomorphic encryption scheme. In *Proc. EUROCRYPT '11*, 2011. DOI: 10.1007/978-3-642-20465-4_9. 31

[46] B. Gedik and L. Liu, "Location privacy in mobile systems. A personalized anonymization model. In *Proc. ICDCS '05*, pages 620–629, 2005. DOI: 10.1109/ICDCS.2005.48. 64

[47] G. Ghinita, P. Kalnis, M. Kantarcioglu, and E. Bertino. A hybrid technique for private location-based queries with database protection. In *Proc. Advances in Spatial and Temporal Databases*, page 98–116, 2009. DOI: 10.1007/978-3-642-02982-0_9. 65

[48] G. Ghinita, P. Kalnis, M. Kantarcioglu, and E. Bertino. Approximate and exact hybrid algorithms for private nearest-neighbor queries with database protection. *GeoInformatica*, 15(4):669–726, 2011. DOI: 10.1007/s10707-010-0121-4. 65, 76

[49] G. Ghinita, P. Kalnis, A. Khoshgozaran, C. Shahabi, and K.-L. Tan. Private queries in location based services: anonymizers are not necessary. In *Proc. SIGMOD '08.*, pages 121–132, 2008. DOI: 10.1145/1376616.1376631. 65, 77

[50] G. Ghinita, C. R. Vicente, N. Shang, and E. Bertino. Privacy-preserving matching of spatial datasets with protection against background knowledge. In *Proc. GIS '10*, pages 3–12, 2010. DOI: 10.1145/1869790.1869795. 81

[51] http://gmplib.org/ 32

[52] O. Goldreich and L. Levin. A hard predicate for all one-way functions. In *Proc. STOC '89*, pages 23–32, 1989. DOI: 10.1145/73007.73010. 2

[53] S. Goldwasser and S. Micali. Probabilistic encryption. *Journal of Computer and Systems Sciences*, 28(2):270–299, 1984. DOI: 10.1016/0022-0000(84)90070-9. 2, 4, 5, 7, 20, 49

[54] M. Green and S. Hohenberger . Blind identity-based encryption and simulatable oblivious transfer. In *Proc. ASIACRYPT '07*, pages 265–282, 2007. DOI: 10.1007/978-3-540-76900-2_16. 17

[55] M. Green and S. Hohenberger . Practical adaptive oblivious transfer from simple assumptions. In *Proc. 8th conference on Theory of cryptography*, pages 347–363, 2011. DOI: 10.1007/978-3-642-19571-6_21. 17

[56] M. Gruteser and D. Grunwald. Anonymous usage of location-based services through spatial and temporal cloaking. In *Proc. 1st international conference on Mobile systems, applications and services*, pp. 31–42, 2003. DOI: 10.1145/1066116.1189037. 64

[57] J. Han and M. Kamber, *Data Mining: Concepts and Techniques*. 2nd Edition. Morgan Kaufmann Publishers, 2006. 37

[58] T. Hashem and L. Kulik. Safeguarding location privacy in wireless ad-hoc networks. In *Proc. UbiComp '07*, pages 372–390, 2007. DOI: 10.1007/978-3-540-74853-3_22. 64

[59] B. Hoh and M. Gruteser, "Protecting location privacy through path confusion," Proc. *SecureComm '05*, 2005, pp. 194–205. DOI: 10.1109/SECURECOMM.2005.33. 64

[60] W. H. Inmon, *Building the Data Warehouse*. John Wiley & Sons, 1996. 37

[61] Y. Ishai and E. Kushilevitz. Improved upper bounds on information theoretic private information retrieval. In *Proc. 31st ACM Symposium on the Theory of Computing*, pp. 79–88, 1999. DOI: 10.1145/301250.301275.

[62] T. Itoh. Efficient private information retrieval. *IEICE Trans. Fund. Electron. Communi. Comput. Sci.* E. 82-A(1), pp. 11–20, 1999.

[63] T. Itoh. On lower bounds for the communication complexity of private information retrieval. *IEICE Trans. Fund. Electron. Communi. Comput. Sci.* E. 84-A(1), pp. 157–164, 2001.

[64] P. Kalnis, G. Ghinita, K. Mouratidis, and D. Papadias. Preventing location-based identity inference in anonymous spatial queries. *IEEE T Knowledge and Data Engineering*, vol. 19, no. 12, pp. 1719–1733, 2007. DOI: 10.1109/TKDE.2007.190662. 64

[65] H. Kido, Y. Yanagisawa, and T. Satoh. An anonymous communication technique using dummies for location-based services. In *Proc. ICPS '05*, pages 88–97, 2005. DOI: 10.1109/PERSER.2005.1506394. 65

[66] J. Krumm. A survey of computational location privacy. *Personal and Ubiquitous Computing*, vol. 13, pp. 391–399, 2009. DOI: 10.1007/s00779-008-0212-5. 65

[67] Kaoru Kurosawa and Ryo Nojima. Simple adaptive oblivious transfer without random oracle. In *Proc. ASIACRYPT '09*, pages 334–346, 2009. DOI: 10.1007/978-3-642-10366-7_20. 17

[68] E. Kushilevitz and R. Ostrovsky. Replication is not needed: Single database, computationally-private information retrieval. In *Proc. 38th Annual IEEE Symposium on the Foundations of Computer Science*, pages 364–373, 1997. DOI: 10.1109/SFCS.1997.646125. 1, 2, 4, 6, 16, 20, 33, 34, 40, 53, 65, 77, 83

[69] E. Kushilevitz and R. Ostrovsky. One-way trapdoor permutations are sufficient for non-trivial single-server private information retrieval. In *Proc. EUROCRYPT '00*, pages 104–121, 2000. DOI: 10.1007/3-540-45539-6_9. 2, 17

[70] Yehuda Lindell. Efficient fully-simulatable oblivious transfer. In *Proc. CT-RSA '08*, pages 52–70, 2008. DOI: 10.1007/978-3-540-79263-5_4. 17

[71] H. Lipmaa. An oblivious transfer protocol with log-squared communication. In *Proc. 8th Information Security Conference*, pages 314–328, 2005. DOI: 10.1007/11556992_23. 2, 20, 33, 34

[72] H. Lipmaa. First CPIR protocol with data-dependent computation. In *Proc. ICISC '09*, pages 193–210, 2009. DOI: 10.1007/978-3-642-14423-3_14. 2

[73] A. Lliev and S. W. Smith. Protecting client privacy with trusted computing at the server. *IEEE Security & Privacy*, 3(2): 20–28, 2005. DOI: 10.1109/MSP.2005.49. 2

[74] L. Marconi, R. Pietro, B. Crispo, and M. Conti. Time warp: how time affects privacy in LBSs. In *Proc. ICICS '10*, pages 325–339, 2010. DOI: 10.1007/978-3-642-17650-0_23. 64

[75] S. Mascetti and C. Bettini. A comparison of spatial generalization algorithms for lbs privacy preservation. In *Proc. 2007 International Conference on Mobile Data Management*, pages 258–262, 2007. DOI: 10.1109/MDM.2007.54. 64

[76] T. Mayberry, E. O. Blass, A. H. Chan. PIRMAP: Efficient private information retrieval for MapReduce. IACR Cryptology ePrint Archive 2012: 398. DOI: 10.1007/978-3-642-39884-1_32. 17

[77] A. Menezes, P. van Oorchot and S. Vanstone, *Handbook of Applied Cryptography*. CRC Press, 1997. 41, 46, 52

[78] S. K. Mishra and P. Sarkar. Symmetrically private information retrieval. In *Proc. INDOCRYPT '00*, pp. 225–236, 2000. DOI: 10.1007/3-540-44495-5_20.

[79] M. F. Mokbel, C.-Y. Chow, and W. G. Aref. The new casper: query processing for location services without compromising privacy. In *Proc. VLDB '06*, pages 763–774, 2006. 64

[80] D. Naccache and J. Stern. A new public key cryptosystem based on higher residues. In *Proc. CCS '98*, pp. 59–66, 1998. DOI: 10.1145/288090.288106. 7

[81] M. Naor and M. Yung. Universal one-way hash functions and their cryptographic applications. In *Proc. STOC '89*, pages 33–43, 1989. DOI: 10.1145/73007.73011. 2

[82] M. Naor and B. Pinkas. Oblivious transfer and polynomial evaluation, In *Proc. STOC '99*, pages 245–254, 1999. DOI: 10.1145/301250.301312. 3, 10, 13

[83] M. Naor and B. Pinkas. Oblivious transfer with adaptive queries. In *Proc. CRYPTO '99*, pages 791–791, 1999. DOI: 10.1007/3-540-48405-1_36. 11, 14, 16, 66, 69, 72, 76

[84] F. Olumofin and I. Goldberg. Revisiting the computational practicality of private information retrieval. Technical Report CACR 2010–17, University of Waterloo, 2010. DOI: 10.1007/978-3-642-27576-0_13. 19

[85] T. Okamoto and S. Uchiyama. A new public-key cryptosystem as secure as factoring. In *Proc. EUROCRYPT '98*, 1998. DOI: 10.1007/BFb0054135. 7, 41

[86] "Openssl," `http://www.openssl.org/`, 2011, [Online; accessed 7-July-2011]. 79

[87] R. Ostovsky and W. E. Skeith III. A survey of single-database PIR: techniques and applications. In *Proc. PKC '07*, pages 393–411, 2007. DOI: 10.1007/978-3-540-71677-8_26. 2, 10, 20

[88] R. Ostrovsky R. and W. E. Skeith III. Private searching on streaming data. In *Proc. Crypto '05*, pages 223–240, 2005. DOI: 10.1007/11535218_14. 83, 84, 85

[89] R. Ostrovsky and W. E. Skeith III. Private searching on streaming data, *Journal of Cryptology*, 20(4), 397–430, 2007. DOI: 10.1007/s00145-007-0565-3. 84, 85

[90] P. Paillier. Public key cryptosystems based on composite degree residue classes. In *Proc. EUROCRYPT '99*, pages 223–238, 1999. DOI: 10.1007/3-540-48910-X_16. 2, 6, 41, 49, 60, 65, 77

[91] B. Palanisamy and L. Liu, Mobimix: Protecting location privacy with mix-zones over road networks. In *Proc. ICDE '11*, pages 494–505, 2011. DOI: 10.1109/ICDE.2011.5767898. 63

[92] R. Paulet, M. G. Kaosar, X. Yi, E. Bertino. Privacy-preserving and content-protecting location based queries. In *Proc. ICDE '12*, pages 44–53, 2012. DOI: 10.1109/ICDE.2012.95. 65, 66, 83

[93] R. Paulet, M. G. Kaosar, X. Yi, E. Bertino. Privacy-preserving and content-protecting location based queries. *IEEE Trans. on Knowledge and Data Eng.*, in press. DOI: 10.1109/ICDE.2012.95. 65, 66, 76, 81, 83

[94] S. Pohlig and M. Hellman. An improved algorithm for computing logarithms over GF(p) and its cryptographic significance. *IEEE Transactions on Information Theory*, 24(1): 106–110, 1978. DOI: 10.1109/TIT.1978.1055817. 2, 9, 77

[95] M. O. Rabin. How to exchange secrets by oblivious transfer. *Technical Report TR-81*, Aiken Computation Laboratory, Harvard University, 1981. 3, 10

[96] R. Rivest, A. Shamir and L. Adleman. A method for obtaining digital signatures and public-key cryptosystems. *Communications of the ACM*, 21 (2): 120–126, 1978. DOI: 10.1145/359340.359342. 49

[97] T. Sander, A. Young and M. Yung. Non-interactive CryptoComputing for NC1. *Proc. 40th Annual Symposium on Foundations of Computer Science*, pages 554–567, 1999. DOI: 10.1109/SFFCS.1999.814630. 30

[98] V. Shoup, "Number thoery library," `http://www.shoup.net/ntl/`, 2009, [Online; accessed 7-July-2011]. 79

[99] R. Sion and B. Carbunar. On the computational practicality of private information retrieval. *Proc. NDSS '07*, 2007. 2

[100] N. Smart and F. Vercauteren. Fully homomorphic encryption with relatively small key and ciphertext sizes. In *Proc. PKC '10*, pages 420–443, 2010. DOI: 10.1007/978-3-642-13013-7_25. 20, 31, 49

[101] D. Stehle and R. Steinfeld. Faster fully homomorphic encryption. In *Proc. ASIACRYPT '10*, pages 377–394, 2010. DOI: 10.1007/978-3-642-17373-8_22. 31

[102] J. Stern. A new and efficient all-or-nothing disclosure of secrets protocol. In *Proc. ASIACRYPT '98*, pp. 357–371, 1998. DOI: 10.1007/3-540-49649-1_28. 10

[103] L. Sweeney. k-anonymity: a model for protecting privacy. *Int. J. Uncertain. Fuzziness Knowl.-Based Syst.*, vol. 10, pp. 557–570, 2002. DOI: 10.1142/S0218488502001648. 64

[104] S. Wang, X. Ding, R. H. Deng and F. Bao. Private information retrieval using trusted hardware. In *Proc. ESORICS '06*, pp. 49–64, 2006. DOI: 10.1007/11863908_4. 2

[105] S. Wiesner. Conjugate coding. *SIGACT News*, pp. 78–88, 1983. DOI: 10.1145/1008908.1008920. 10

[106] X. Yi, M. Kaosar, R. Paulet and E. Bertino. Single-database private information retrieval from fully homomorphic encryption. *IEEE Trans. on Knowledge and Data Eng.*, 25(5): 1125–1134, 2013. DOI: 10.1109/TKDE.2012.90. 20, 21, 23, 24, 26, 27, 31, 32, 34, 35, 40, 53, 83

[107] X. Yi, R. Paulet and E. Bertino. Private data warehouse queries. In *Proc. SACMAT '13*, pages 25–36, 2013. DOI: 10.1145/2462410.2462418. 40, 42, 45, 50, 83

[108] X. Yi and E. Bertino. Private searching for single and conjunctive keywords on streaming data. In *Proc. WPES '11*, pages 153–158, 2011. DOI: 10.1145/2046556.2046577. 85

[109] X. Yi and C. P. Xing. Private (t, n) threshold searching on streaming data. In *Proc. SocialCom/PASSAT'12*, pages 676–683, 2012. DOI: 10.1109/SocialCom-PASSAT.2012.47. 85

[110] T. Xu and Y. Cai. Feeling-based location privacy protection for location-based services. In *Proc. CCS '09*, pages 348–357, 2009. DOI: 10.1145/1653662.1653704. 64

Authors' Biographies

XUN YI

Xun Yi is a professor with the College of Engineering and Science, Victoria University, Australia. His research interests include applied cryptography, computer and network security, mobile and wireless communication security, and privacy-preserving data mining. He has published more than 100 research papers in international journals, such as *IEEE Trans. Knowledge and Data Engineering, IEEE Trans. Wireless Communication, IEEE Trans. Dependable and Secure Computing, IEEE Trans. Circuit and Systems, IEEE Trans. Vehicular Technologies, IEEE Communication Letters, IEE Electronic Letters,* and conference proceedings. He has undertaken program committee members for more than 20 international conferences. He is leading a few of Australia Research Council (ARC) Discovery Projects.

RUSSELL PAULET

Russell Paulet is currently studying for a PhD degree at Victoria University in Melbourne, Australia. He holds an undergraduate degree in Computer Science and associated Honours degree from Victoria University. His Honours thesis was in the field of Image Processing, specifically dealing with atmospheric noise such as rain. The subject of his PhD is cryptography and computer privacy, which is supervised by Dr. Xun Yi and co-supervised by Dr. Alasdair McAndrew. His research interests include cryptography, data mining and privacy-preserving data mining, applied mathematics, and computer protocols.

ELISA BERTINO

Elisa Bertino is a professor with the Computer Science Department at Purdue University and serves as research director of CERIAS. Previously, she was a faculty member in the Department of Computer Science and Communication of the University of Milan. Her main research interests include security, privacy, digital identity management systems, database systems, distributed systems, and multimedia systems. She is a fellow of the IEEE and a fellow of the ACM. She received the 2002 IEEE Computer Society Technical Achievement Award for outstanding contributions to database systems and database security and advanced data management systems and the 2005 IEEE Computer Society Tsutomu Kanai Award for pioneering and innovative research contributions to secure distributed systems.